RUNNING AFTER GOD

"The Ultimate Pursuit"

"My soul followeth hard after thee..."
Psalm 63:8

Dr. Josie Carr

Tulsa, OK

Unless otherwise indicated, all Scripture quotations are taken from the *King James Version* of the Bible.

Scripture quotations marked NKJV are taken from the *New King James Version*®. Copyright © 1982 by Thomas Nelson, Inc. Used by permission. All rights reserved.

Scripture quotations marked MSG are taken from *The Message*. Copyright © 1993, 1994, 1995, 1996, 2000, 2001, 2002. Used by permission of NavPress Publishing Group.

Scripture quotations marked NIV are taken from the HOLY BIBLE, NEW INTERNATIONAL VERSION®. Copyright © 1973, 1978, 1984 by International Bible Society. Used by permission of Zondervan. All rights reserved.

Scripture quotations marked ESV are taken from the *ESV*® *Bible* (The Holy Bible, English Standard Version®), copyright © 2001 by Crossway, a publishing ministry of Good News Publishers. Used by permission. All rights reserved.

Scripture quotations marked NLT are taken from the *Holy Bible, New Living Translation*, copyright © 1996, 2004, 2007 by Tyndale House Foundation. Used by permission of Tyndale House Publishers, Inc., Carol Stream, Illinois 60188. All rights reserved.

Scripture quotations marked AMP are taken from the *Amplified Bible*, copyright © 1954, 1958, 1962, 1964, 1965, 1987 by The Lockman Foundation. Used by permission. (www.Lockman.org)

18 17 16 15 10 9 8 7 6 5 4 3 2 1

Running After God: The Ultimate Pursuit
ISBN 13: 978-168031-039-9
Copyright © 2015 by Dr. Josie Carr
Spring, TX 77379
Published by Harrison House Publishers
Tulsa, OK 74145
www.harrisonhouse.com

Printed in the United States of America. All rights reserved under International Copyright Law. Contents and/or cover may not be reproduced in whole or in part in any form without the express written consent of the Publisher.

DEDICATION

To my family; Stan, Jarvis, and Jakia.

Continue in the way of the Lord. Trust and obey Him.
Follow hard after Him.

I thank God for you daily. You have truly been my inspiration and the quiet forces behind the scenes. Thank you for believing in me and allowing me to fulfill the purpose of God for my life.

I love you, always!

TABLE OF CONTENTS

Introduction 1
Lesson Plan 5
Scope and Sequence 7

Week 1- General Session - To Know Him 9
   Independant Study - To Know Him 13
      Day 1—"The Trinity" 14
      Day 2—"God - The Father" 18
      Day 3—"God – The Father, Part 2" 23
      Day 4—"God - The Son" 29
      Day 5—"God - The Holy Spirit" 34

Week 2- General Session - Intimacy with God 39
   Independant Study - Intimacy with God 43
      Day 1—"His Workmanship" 44
      Day 2—"God - "Student of the Word" 49
      Day 3—"Prayer" 53
      Day 4—"Praise" 57
      Day 5—"Worship" 61

Week 3 - General Session - Are You in Idolatry 65
   Independant Study - Are You in Idolatry 71
      Day 1—"A Jealous God" 72
      Day 2—"Disobedience" 76
      Day 3—"Identifying the Idols" 81
      Day 4—"Getting Rid of Idols" 87
      Day 5—"Focus on God (F.O.G.)" 90

Week 4 - General Session -Divine Treasure Hunt 95
   Independant Study - Divine Treasure Hunt 99

- Day 1—"Wisdom" 100
- Day 2—"Wisdom" 105
- Day 3—"Pearls of Great Price" 108
- Day 4—"Potential Pearls" 112
- Day 5—"Grace" 116

Week 5 - General Session - Surrender 121
- Independant Study - Surrender 125
- Day 1—"Thirst" 126
- Day 2—"Thirst" 130
- Day 3—"Hunger" 134
- Day 4—"Spending Time with God" 138
- Day 5—"Hearing His Voice" 144

Week 6 - General Session - Reflections 149
- Day 1—"Arise and Shine" 153
- Day 2—"Light" 157
- Day 3—"Love" 161
- Day 4—"Love – Your Neighbor" 166
- Day 5—"Love – Yourself" 170

About the Author 177

INTRODUCTION

In today's culture, people are pursuing many things. It has become popular to "pursue your passion," "pursue success," "pursue wealth," "pursue what makes you happy." While all of this is wonderful, I have discovered none of these things promote ultimate fulfillment nor do they have a positive eternal impact. The only pursuit that ends in ultimate fulfillment is the pursuit of God and His plan for our lives.

The unique thing about pursuing God is what happens when you find Him. An amazing discovery is that it is He who has been pursuing you. You will discover that He loves you beyond description and articulation. You will find it difficult to pursue Him and just walk away. His love and mercy toward you will keep you running after Him more and more. He is incredible! As you pursue God, you will fall deeply in love with Him as He is with you. This is a love affair that NEVER ends.

When first impressed to do Bible studies that would help women be all they could be and do all they could do according to God's will for their lives, I knew God wanted me to study pursuing Him simply because that was His desire for me…to continue running after Him with all my might.

Recently, I was in a meeting where Julie Meyer ministered the Word of God. Upon completion of her message, she called for people to come to the altar for a time of worship and prayer. She began to lay hands on the people and when she got to me, she laid hands, prayed, and moved on. Then, she backed up, came to me again and said "God is calling you Josie. He's saying come up higher, come up higher." She began to prophesy about my family and some things God was going to do there. Later she said God was going to use me and give me a name in the city in which I live.

Since that day, my pursuit for God (the things of God) has gotten stronger. I want to please Him with, and in, all I do. This may sound a little bizarre to you, but I am falling in love with Him, more and more. He is so awesome!

In my pursuit of Him, I have discovered that prayer, praise and worship are key components to intimacy with Him. When we spend time in praise and worship, it focuses our minds on Him. It gives Him a place to dwell, and it opens heavenly portals over us that release His presence. We begin to hear clearer, see farther, and get answers to our daily dilemmas.

The Word is another major component of running after God. The Scriptures testify of Him. They inform us of who He is and His will and His way, as well as His unconditional love for us. The Word of God reveals His desire for us to make Him the focus of our pursuit.

Running after God simply means getting to know Him, having intimacy with Him, putting no one and nothing above Him. It means total surrender to Him. It means getting up when you have fallen down. It means not quitting when you have made a mistake. It means repenting when you have violated His Word. It means pleasing Him is the objective and purpose for everything you do.

There are several examples from the Word that highlight others who ran after God. As you read these accounts, you will realize what they did—you can do as well. You may think you are not holy enough or good enough for such a pursuit, but that is not so my friend. Your past is just that; it is your past. You must forget the past and focus on the present and future that God has for you. In Philippians 3:13-14, Paul writes: **"Brethren, I do not count myself to have apprehended; but one thing I do, forgetting those things which are behind and reaching forward to those things which are ahead. I press toward**

the goal of the high calling of God in Christ Jesus" (NKJV). Jeremiah 29:11 assures you that God has thoughts of peace towards you to give you hope and a future. Hallelujah!

In the scriptures, we see that God referred to David as a man after His own heart (Acts 13:22 and I Samuel 13:14). Amidst all of David's mistakes and mishaps in I Kings 14:8, God said David kept His commandments and *followed* Him with all his heart to do that only which was right in His eyes. First Samuel 16:7 says that the Lord does not see as man sees; for man looks at the outward appearance, but God looks at the heart.

I researched the word "followed" in the dictionary and found to my pleasant amazement that it means to: pursue, be guided by, accept the guidance of; imitate; obey; stick to and observe closely. That says it all....it is as plain as day! You are to pursue God, be guided by Him, imitate Him, obey Him and observe Him closely with ALL of your heart! This is a perfect example of a person in hot pursuit of their lover. After all, isn't Jesus the lover of your soul?

Abraham is another example of one who ran after God. He was a God chaser indeed. His chief joy was to obey God. Abraham believed God and it was counted unto him as righteousness (Romans 4:3). Whatever God instructed him to do, he did without question. When God told Abraham to leave his family and He would show him where to go (Genesis 12:1-9), Abraham did not question God; he obeyed Him. When God told him to sacrifice his only son (Genesis 22:1-12), he did not hesitate; he obeyed.

Of course you know we have the greatest example of all—Jesus. He had a zeal for God. He was passionate about seeking the Father and obeying His every command. Even as a young boy, Jesus was found saying, "I must be about My Father's business" (Luke 2:49, NKJV).

Often, He would slip away from the multitudes to spend quality time with the Father (Matthew 14:22, 23). He and the Father had an intimate relationship. Jesus did nothing outside of the Father's will. Even when obeying God was difficult in the flesh, Jesus said, "Not my will, but thine be done" (Luke 22: 39-46). Wow!

My friend, God has called you and me to this very same passionate pursuit, to know and obey Him, and to make Him bigger than anything else in our lives. A thirst for more of Him should drive us to a deeper and more intimate relationship with Him. The mantra of our lives should echo the words of King David in Psalm 63:8, "My soul follows hard after thee."

As we approach this Bible study, I am humbled to be used of God as your teacher. Teaching is my passion and vocation. However, I've learned—both professionally and spiritually—that it carries an enormous price tag. A good teacher always becomes a part of the lesson he or she teaches. There has to be an "on-purpose" connection and for that reason, I approached this study with much prayer, fasting and research.

I urge you to not just go through the motions, but to become a part of the quest to pursue God…to run after Him with all your heart. Focus on Him. Hear what He is saying to you in this season. I believe He will take you places you have never been in Him and He will show you things you have never seen.

Are you ready? Be sure your shoelaces are tied because you are in for an exhilarating experience! **Running After God - The Ultimate Pursuit** is not only a six week event, it is a lifelong marathon. I am glad that we are taking this run together.

I love you,
Dr. Carr

Lesson Plan

❖ Our study will cover six weeks, each with five days of independent study/homework.

❖ Lessons are broken into two segments: **General Session (GS)** and **Independent Study (IS)**.

❖ General Session will consist of:

1. Opening prayer and greeting

2. A 30-minute review of Independent Study from the previous week

3. Questions/concerns/discussion from previous lesson (only)

4. Lesson presentation and focus for next week

5. Independent Study reminder

❖ Independent Study will consist of:

1. Support lessons that students will engage in during the week

2. Information to read and comprehension questions to complete

3. Answers that are not right or wrong, but used for dialogue and discussion

As discussion occurs, I believe Holy Spirit will bring the necessary revelation and correction, as needed.

❖ The first week of each study (except teleconference classes) will include:

1. Meet and greet

2. Purchase of book(s)

3. Introduction to study

SCOPE AND SEQUENCE

Running After God – The Ultimate Pursuit

Week	Day 1	Day 2	Day 3	Day 4	Day 5
• Introduction • Purchase of Books • Meet and Greet	5 min.	Prayer 5 min.	Festival 5 min.	Week 5 min.	5 min.
1 To Know Him	The Trinity	God the Father	God the Father - II	God the Son	God the Holy Spirit
2 Intimacy with God	His Workmanship	Student of the Word	Prayer	Praise	Worship
3 Are You in Idolatry	A Jealous God	Disobedience	Identifying the Idols	Getting Rid of Idols	Focus on God (F.O.G.)
4 Divine Treasure Hunt	Wisdom	Wisdom	Pearls of Great Price	Potential Pearls	Grace
5 Total Surrender	Thirst	Thirst	Hunger	Spending Time with God	Hearing His Voice
6 Reflections	Arise and Shine	Light	Love	Love Your Neighbor	Love Yourself
Wrap – Up Final Review Gathering		Focus	On	Worship	

Week 1
GENERAL SESSION

To Know Him

"And I will give them a heart to know me, that I am the LORD: and they shall be my people, and I will be their God: for they shall return unto me with their whole heart."
Jeremiah 24:7

GENERAL SESSION
To Know Him

God wants us to know Him, not just know of Him. He wants us to go beyond just knowing He exists to truly knowing Him intimately as *Abba* Father.

I was praying this morning as I was driving on the freeway and asked God what His heart's desire was for today. He spoke back and said, "My heart's desire is that My people would know Me, because if they really knew Me and how much I love them, they would not fear. They would not give up. They would do great exploits, and if they really knew Me, they would take the limits off because in Me, there are no limits."

I was really taken by His response because that's our topic for this week and because I could sense that God was sort of grieved by the fact that we don't really know Him or at least, we don't act as if we do. Additionally, I had a sense that we will never be able to do those greater works that Jesus talked about until we really KNOW HIM and abandon all excuses and limitations. God is limitless and we are to live like it, love like it, and be about His business like it.

Let's look at Scripture text:

Jeremiah 24:7: **"And I will give them a heart to KNOW me, that I am the LORD: and they shall be my people, and I will be their God: for they shall return unto me with their whole heart"** (emphasis mine).

Daniel 11:32: **"But the people that do know their God, shall be strong and do exploits."** In the NKJV, it says, **"The people who know**

their God shall be strong, and carry out _great_ exploits" (emphasis mine).

I believe from the day you were born, you have been on a quest. You have been searching for something more because deep down inside, you have a sense that life must have some kind of meaning and purpose beyond mere existence.

Whether you are young or old, rich or poor, male or female, black or white— you were designed to KNOW God in a deep and personal way.

Some might ask, "How do I know God?"

- ❖ You know God by salvation through Jesus Christ (Romans 10: 9-10). **"Neither is there salvation in any other: for there is none other name under heaven given among men, whereby we must be saved"** (Acts 4:12).

- ❖ You know God by the Word. **"Search the scriptures; for in them ye think ye have eternal life; and they are they which testify of me"** (John 5:39). **"In the beginning was the Word…and the Word was God"** (John 1:1).

- ❖ You know God by fellowshipping with Him—spending quality time with God in prayer, praise, and worship, having conversation with Him, being thankful for all He has done and is doing, and adoring and reverencing Him for Who He is.

God created you. He loves you so much that He wants you to know Him now and to spend eternity with Him. Jesus said, **"For God so loved the world that He gave His only begotten Son"** (John 3:16). Jesus came so that we can know God.

Now in getting to know God, there is also a seeking involved. We have to seek Him or pursue Him. Jeremiah 29:13 says, **"And you will seek Me and find Me, when you search for Me with all your heart"** (NKJV).

The floor is open for dialogue. Let's talk.

1. What does it mean to you to KNOW GOD?

   _____

   _____

   _____

2. In Romans 1:19-21, it speaks of nature testifying of God. Is simply believing that you know God and that He exists because of what you see in nature enough to sustain a powerful relationship with Him? Explain your answer.

   _____

   _____

   _____

3. What does Daniel 11:32 mean to you? Are you doing great exploits?

   _____

   _____

   _____

INDEPENDENT STUDY

To Know Him

"And I will give them a heart to know me, that I am the LORD: and they shall be my people, and I will be their God: for they shall return unto me with their whole heart."
Jeremiah 24:7

Week *One*

To Know Him

Day 1—"The Trinity"

- ❖ "Hear, O Israel: The LORD our God, the LORD is one!" (Deuteronomy 6:4, NKJV)
- ❖ "I am the LORD, and there is no other; There is no God besides Me." (Isaiah 45:5, NKJV)
- ❖ "There is no other God but one." (1 Corinthians 8:4, NKJV)

God the Father, God the Son and God the Holy Spirit make up what we call the trinity. The word "trinity" is made up of two words: "tri," meaning three and "unity," meaning one. God is three persons with the same distinct essence of deity. God the Son, Jesus, is completely God. God the Spirit, Holy Spirit, is completely God. God the Father is completely God.

The word trinity is not found in the scriptures, however, the concept is taught there. Genesis 1:26, contains the plural pronouns "us" and "our." This is referring to the trinity. God exists as three persons (Father, Son, and Holy Ghost), not as three separate gods. Remember, the Lord is one!

Jesus is referred to as God a number of times in the Bible. Where would we find such a reference? In John 1:3 or John 20:28?

_____

In the space provided, write out Colossians 2:9.

_____

_____

_____

_____

First John 5:20 says, **"And we know that the Son of God is come, and hath given us an understanding, that we may know him that is true, even in his Son Jesus Christ. This is the _____ _____ and _____ _____."**

Jesus is referred to as the "Mighty God" in the Old Testament. We can find this scripture in Isaiah chapter 9 and verse _____.

We know, according to John 1:1, that the Word was in the beginning and the Word was with God and the Word was God. In your own words, what is this scripture saying to us?

_____

_____

_____

_____

Read John 17:5. Explain what Jesus meant when he said "before the world was."

_____

_____

_____

_____

Read Revelation 5:11-14. Is this scripture referring to God the Father, God the Son, or God the Holy Spirit? _____

_____

Is it safe to say that Jesus receives the same worship and honor as does God the Father? _____ YES _____ NO

As we focus on the Holy Spirit, He is often referred to as "the Spirit of God" in both Old and New Testaments. The Holy Spirit is not part God; He is God.

When we look at Genesis chapter one, we see that "in the beginning," the Holy Spirit was there. Read Genesis 1:2 and fill in the blanks. **"And the _____ _____ _____ moved upon the face of the waters."**

People normally find it easy to understand Jesus as being God, because He had a human experience which included a body. The Scriptures make it quite clear that Jesus was obviously a person with experiences like us. However, the Holy Spirit never had a physical body and He is symbolized as a dove, wind, or breath in the Scripture. This has caused some to think of Him as an "it," or as vague and less important. Yet, this is not the case at all! The Holy Spirit is a person; He has personality and feelings. And He is God.

In his writings, Paul speaks of the power of God, the power of Christ, and the power of the Holy Spirit. Also in I Corinthians 12, the subject of the verse changes from God in verse 6, to the Spirit in verse 11. Look at Acts 5:3 below. Underline who Peter said Ananias lied to.

"But Peter said, Ananias why hath Satan filled thine heart to lie to the Holy Ghost, and to keep back part of the price of the land?"

Now read Acts 5:4. Fill in the blank:

"...thou has not lied unto men, but unto _____."

I am sure you will conclude with me that there is one triune God—God the Father, God the Son, and God the Holy Spirit. For the remainder of this week, we will study the distinct attributes and names of the Father, Son, and Holy Spirit.

Week *One*

To Know Him

Day 2—"God - The Father"

"And this is life eternal, that they might know thee the only true God."

John 17:3

In our General Session, we discussed God's desire for us to know Him. We looked at scripture such as Jeremiah 24:7 that tells us that God has given us a heart to know Him and to know that He is Lord. As we said earlier in our discussion, there is an intrinsic desire in all of us to know God.

Today, we are going to go deeper into knowing God as we get a revelation of who He is by studying His names. Each name paints a beautiful portrait of Him and reveals a precious promise from Him. Each conveys His character, His ways and what He means to us.

In Scripture, a person's name identified him and stood for something specific. This is especially true of God. There are several accounts in the Bible where God changed a person's name to represent the character He wanted him to reflect. For example, when God wanted Abram, which meant "high father," to see himself as "father of many," He changed his name to Abraham (Genesis 17:5). When He wanted Sarai, "my princess," to see herself as "mother of nations," He changed her name to Sarah (Genesis 17:15). When He wanted Jacob, "supplanter," to see himself as "having power with God," He changed his name to Israel (Genesis 32:28). There are other names in the Bible that were changed as well. Can you think of one? I'll give you a hint. Look at John 1:42. Fill in the blanks:

_____'s name was changed to _____

which is interpreted _____

Read 1 Samuel 25:25. What does the name Nabal mean?

_____

_____

Allow the following scripture to serve as a backdrop for the remainder of our time together today:

Psalm 148:13: **"Let them praise the name of the LORD:** *for his name alone is excellent;* **his glory is above the earth and heaven"** (emphasis added).

Let's look at several Hebrew names for God. I have provided scripture references to encourage further study of this subject matter. It is necessary to research the "further study" scriptures for our discussion. Additionally, you may want to visit www.biblegateway.com for a more concentrated study of these names. Most of the following names are referenced from the above website.

El – This name for God, including pagan or false gods, derived from a root word that means might, strength and power. However, when referring to the God of Israel (our God), it is qualified by additional words that further express and define the meaning, which distinguishes Him (our God) from false gods. This word "El" appears in the Bible over 250 times.

Elohim – This is the plural of El (inferring the trinity) and is the first name for God that is given in the Bible. Genesis 1:1 states, **"In the beginning, God (Elohim) created the heavens and the earth."**

Elohim means "God." Further study scriptures include Jeremiah 32:27; Deuteronomy 5:23, 8:15; Psalm 68:7.

El Olam – The Everlasting God; The Ancient of Days; The Eternal God. The God who is unchangeable and inexhaustible! El Olam is a combination of two words, "El" which simply means God and "Olam," which literally means forever. Further study scriptures include Genesis 21:33; Jeremiah 10:10; Psalm 90: 1-3, 93:2; Isaiah 26:4.

El Elyon – The Most High God. This name denotes God's strength, sovereignty, and supremacy (Genesis 14:20; Psalm 9:2). He surpasses all others. He is greater than the greatest and mightier than the mightiest! None can compare to El Elyon, He is MOST HIGH! Hallelujah? Hallelujah! The single form of the name, Elyon, occurs in 2 Samuel 22:14 and Psalm 7:17. Further study scriptures include Daniel 3:26, 4:34; Deuteronomy 32:8; Psalm 78:35.

El Roi – The God Who Sees (Genesis 16:7-13; Exodus 3:7). If God sees all, we can infer that nothing surprises Him or catches Him off-guard. God is never in a panic mode trying to figure out what to do because we disobeyed Him. Our ways are before Him and He watches all our paths. That means He knows where you are, what you are doing, and what you are going through. Further study scriptures include Proverbs 5:21, 15:3; Psalm 11:4; Hebrews 4:13.

El Qanna – (pronounced kan-naw') The Jealous God. The primary meaning relates to a marriage, God as Israel's husband. This name also suggests that God watches over us lovingly and closely. This name is first depicted in Exodus chapter 20. Further study scriptures include Numbers 5:14; Deuteronomy 4:24; Josiah 24:19; Joel 2:18.

El Shaddai – All Sufficient God and Lord God Almighty. Genesis 17:1 literally says "I am El Shaddai; walk before me, and be thou perfect." In Genesis 49:25, the name is closely related to the Hebrew word shadaim, indicating sufficiency or nourishment—blessings of the breasts and of the womb. This name may have also gotten its origin from the contraction sha which means who, and dai which means enough. Further study scriptures include Genesis 28:3, 35: 11, 49:25.

Adonai – (pronounced Ad-o-noy') Adonai is plural, the singular is Adon. Adon can, and in most cases, does refer to men, but Adonai refers to God only (Genesis 15:2). Though in its plural form, it is not suggesting that we have three Gods, but rather highlighting the fact that our God is triune: Father, Son, and Holy Spirit. Adonai is more than a name, it depicts a relationship. He is Lord, Master, Ruler, and Owner, and we are His total possession, workmanship and creation. Therefore, we must give Him total surrender. If we call Him Lord, we must live like He is Lord. The phrase "He is Lord" must go beyond our lips and be evident in the way we live. We only deceive ourselves when we call Him Lord and don't do the things he says. Further study scriptures include Psalm 9:10: Isaiah 6:1-8; Joshua 5:13-15; Luke 6:46.

Are you getting this? Let's stop here and test for understanding.

Why did God change Sarai's name? _____

_____

_____

The names of God convey His _____,

_____ and _____.

What Hebrew name describes a father with breasts? _____

Match the following:

NAMES OF GOD	**SCRIPTURE SUPPORT**
___Elohim	A. Psalm 91:1
___El Olam	B. I Corinthians 6:19
___El Shaddai	C. Isaiah 26:4
___Adonai	D. Isaiah 45:18

My friend, it has been fun out on the track with you again today. We will stop here and continue with the names of God tomorrow.

Cheers!

Week *One*

To Know Him

Day 3—"God – The Father, Part 2"

It's a great day to be alive and on the track running after God. As I sit in my hotel room and reflect on the awesomeness of God, my soul leaps with excitement. His name alone is enormous. When I think in terms of my name, It is just Josie. But God, the Father—El, Elohim, Adonai, El Elyon, and more. Our God is huge and there is none that can compare to Him. Buddah, Mohammed…..nay…no match for the MOST HIGH! He trumps them all!

We will continue our run today with the names of God. Let's warm up before we get out there. Review the list of names from yesterday and complete the following:

NAME	DESCRIPTION
El Elyon	_____
Elohim	_____
El Shaddai	_____

Great job! You will find that knowing the names of God gives you a clearer picture of Him and takes your prayers, praise, worship, and expectations to another level.

Read Psalm 138:1-2:

"I will praise thee with my whole heart: before the gods will I sing praise unto thee. I will worship toward thy holy temple,

and praise thy name for thy lovingkindness and for thy truth: for thou hast magnified thy word above all thy name."

Now read this scripture in The Message Bible:

"Thank you! Everything in me says 'Thank you!' Angels listen as I sing my thanks. I kneel in worship facing your holy temple and say it again: 'Thank you!' Thank you for your love, thank you for your faithfulness; Most holy is your name, most holy is your Word. The moment I called out, you stepped in; you made my life large with strength."

In reference to God's name, what does this scripture mean to you?

_____

_____

_____

As we continue with the names of God, keep in mind that a name was not only identification but identity as well.

Jah – (pronounced Yah) This is a short form of the Hebrew title Jehovah (Lord). This name only appears once in the King James Version of the Bible. It is found in Psalm 68:4.

Jehovah – (Lord) "The Existing One" – derived from the Hebrew word *Havah*, meaning "to be," specifically, "to be known." This is the special name that God referred to when speaking to Moses at the burning bush. Read Exodus 3:14-15. This name declares God's absolute being. He is the source of everything. Further study scripture is Exodus 6:3.

Jehovah Tsidkenu – (pronounced tsid-kay'-noo) Tsedek, from which Tsidkenu is derived, means to be "straight" or "righteous." Combined, this name is translated, The Lord our Righteousness. Further study scripture is Jeremiah 23:6, 33:16.

Jehovah M'Kaddesh – (pronounced M-qadash) The Lord Who Sanctifies and the Lord Who Makes Holy. M'Kaddesh (a variant spelling) is derived from a Hebrew word meaning "sanctify," "holy," or "dedicate." To be sanctified is to be set apart for something. You are set apart and dedicated to God. Jehovah M'Kaddesh is the Lord who sets you apart for His purposes. Further study scriptures include Exodus 31:13; Leviticus 20:8.

Jehovah Shammah – (pronounced shaw'- maw) The Lord Who Is There. This name was derived from the Hebrew word sham, which is translated as "there." It was a symbolic name for the earthly Jerusalem. It indicated that God would not abandon His people and leave them in their troubles standing alone, but He would be right there in the midst with them and would restore them to wholeness. He is Jehovah Shammah for you today. Wherever you are in life, Jehovah Shammah is there. He *is* the fourth man in the fire! He *is* in the midst of you and He will restore you to wholeness. Further study scripture is Ezekiel 48:35.

I have a question for you: Are you feeling this? I mean, I am about to come unglued here. The love that exudes from God's names is exhilarating, comforting and peaceful. It supports the scripture in 1 John 4:18 that says "perfect love casts out fear."

Write what you are feeling as you study the names of God, the Father.

_____

_____

Let's move on, as there are a few more names that we want to spotlight during our study today.

Jehovah Shalom – (pronounced shaw-lome') The Lord our Peace. This name was ascribed to God in Judges 6:23-24. It is derived from the Hebrew word *shalem* which means "be complete," or "sound," or "whole." Shalom is translated as peace or absence from strife. It means total wholeness, nothing missing and nothing broken. Hallelujah! Further study scriptures include Psalm 29:11; Philippians 4:7-8; Isaiah 26:3.

Jehovah Rapha – (pronounced raw-faw') The Lord our Healer. This name is first mentioned in Exodus 15:26. In Hebrew, *rapha* means "to restore," "to heal," and "to make healthful." Indeed, He is the Great Physician who heals us physically, mentally, and emotionally. This means you don't give up if you receive a bad report from the doctor. No, that's the time to press in to who He is. He *is* the God who heals every kind of sickness and disease. There is nothing too difficult for Him. Further study scriptures include Jeremiah 30:17, 3:22; Isaiah 61:1; Psalm 103:3.

Jehovah Jireh – (pronounced yir-eh') – The Lord our Provider. This is a symbolic name that Abraham gave on Mount Moriah in honor to God for providing a substitute sacrifice for his son Isaac. Jireh translates into "provide," which has great Latin roots as well. "Pro" means before and "video" means to see. The full translation means to see in advance or before the need is known. Isn't this good news? You see, God knew exactly what you would need at this moment in your life and, here's the amazing part, He provided for it ahead of time. It is already done!

To Know Him

Case closed! Every need you have is met in the name of Jesus! Further study scriptures include Genesis 22:1-14; I Peter 1:3; Philippians 4:19.

Let's take a look at Genesis 22:1-14. How would you best answer the following questions?

Did Abraham expect God to provide a sacrifice for his son?

____YES ____NO

Explain your answer_____

_____

_____

_____

_____

Describe Isaac's attitude in verse 7. _____

What was the sacrifice that God provided for Isaac? _____

_____

Where did you find your answer? _____

We are on our last lap for today. You began well, so I know you want to finish well. Be sure to breathe!

Jehovah Saboath – (pronounced se-ba-ot) The Lord of Hosts (Armies). This name denotes God's universal sovereignty over every army, both spiritual and earthly. He is the King of all heaven and earth, the Mighty Commander and Chief. Further study scriptures include I Samuel 1:3, 17:45; Psalm 24:9-10, 84:3; Isaiah 6:5.

Jehovah Nissi – (pronounced nis-see) The Lord our Banner, The Lord our Miracle. The word *Nissi* was derived from the Hebrew word Nes, which means banner. Moses ascribed this name to the altar at Rephidim, after the Lord gave Joshua and the children of Israel the ability to defeat the Amelikites. The victory came as Moses lifted the rod of God in the air. As long as Moses' hand was up, Israel prevailed. However, when Moses became weak and his arm fell, the Amelikites prevailed. Moses' rod represented the Word of God (Jesus). It was an ensign that encouraged the people to remember their God who always gave them the victory. He is the One who gave them miracle after miracle. Jehovah Nissi is His name! Further study scriptures include Exodus 17:8-16; Psalm 91:1-16; 2 Corinthians 2:14.

Jehovah Raah – (pronounced raw-aw) The Lord our Shepherd. Variant spelling: Jehovah Ro'he. Roeh from which Raah derived, means "shepherd" in Hebrew. A shepherd is one who feeds or leads His flock to pasture. An extension of this translated would be the word rea, which means friend or companion, which indicates the intimacy that God desires between Himself and His people. The two words combined, Jehovah Raah, could also be translated as "The Lord our Friend." Further study scriptures include Psalm 23:1, 80:1 Genesis 48:15, 49:24.

Use one of the names above and give an example of how the Father recently expressed Himself to you in that way.

_____

_____

_____

Week *One*

To Know Him

Day 4—"God - The Son"

"For unto us a child is born, unto us a son is given: and the government shall be upon his shoulder: and his name shall be called Wonderful, Counselor, The mighty God, The everlasting Father, The Prince of Peace."

Isaiah 9:6

"And she (Mary) will bring forth a son; and you shall call His name Jesus, for He will save His people from their sins." **(explanation mine)**

Matthew 1:21

Today on our run, we will spotlight Jesus. He is God, the Son! Matthew 16: 16 states, **"And Simon Peter answered and said, Thou art the Christ, the Son of the living God."**

The name "Jesus" is derived from the Hebrew-Aramaic word Yeshua, meaning Yahweh (the Lord) is salvation. The name "Christ" is actually a title for Jesus. It comes from the Greek word Christos, meaning the Anointed One, or Messiah in Hebrew.

The chart below highlights a few of the names and titles of Jesus. Review it and commit at least one title, meaning and Bible reference to memory. For example, I chose the title, **Word**. It means "Jesus revealed God." It is found in John 1:1 which says: **"In the beginning was the Word, and the Word was with God, and the Word was God."** Now, you choose one.

Title	Meaning/Significance of Names	Bible Reference
Son of God	The special relationship of Jesus to God	Mark 1:1
Son of Man	The human identity of Jesus	Matthew 8:20
Son of David	Jesus is a descendant of King David	Matthew 15:22
Word	Jesus revealed God	John 1:1
Lamb of God	Jesus is the sacrifice for the world's sin	John 1:29
Christ	Greek for 'Anointed One'	Matthew 16:16
Savior	The one who saves	John 4:14
Rabbi/Teacher	Jesus taught people about God	John 1:38, Mark 5:35
Author of Life	One who gives life	Acts 3:15
Alpha and Omega	The first and last letters of the Greek alphabets, meaning that Jesus is the beginning and the end	Revelation 1:8
Lion of Judah	A title of the Messiah	Revelation 5:5
King of Kings/ Lord of Lords	The ruler of all people	Revelation 19:16
Bright Morning Star	The one who gives light	Revelation 22:16
Word of God	Jesus is the voice of God	Revelation 19:13
Holy and Righteous	Attributes of Jesus	Acts 3:14
Head of the Church	The leader of all Christians	Ephesians 5:23

To Know Him

Which one did you choose?

_____

_____

_____

There are many names by which Jesus is known. Each denotes the divine nature of His life, ministry, message, and mandate. Each gives you a glimpse of His awesomeness and glory. As you muse over these names, I pray that your understanding is enriched and your desire for more of Him to be expressed through you is increased.

Jesus is your:

Advocate	Stands before God on your behalf	I John 2:1
Bread	Necessary food	John 6:32
Chief Cornerstone	Force on which our faith is based	Ephesians 2:19-20
Door	The only way to salvation	John 10:9
Emmanuel	God with us	Matthew 1:23
Foundation	Sure foundation	1 Corinthians 3:11
Good Shepherd	He guides by showing the way	John 10:11
High Priest	The one true sacrifice for sin	Hebrews 4:14
I Am	Eternal, timeless, and unchanging	John 8:58

Cite another scripture that refers to Jesus as "I Am." Circle your answer.

    a. I Peter 2:24

    b. Philippians 4:19

    c. John 11:25

    d. Genesis 1:1

Judge	He will judge the righteous	2 Timothy 4:8
King of kings	His supreme rule will be displayed	Revelation 19:16
Lord of lords	He is superior in power and authority	Revelation 19:16
Mediator	The middleman between God and man	I Timothy 2:5
Physician	He heals and delivers	Luke 5:31
Rabbi	Teacher, master	John 3:2
Saviour	Delivers people from sin	Luke 2:11
Truth	The ultimate reality in the earth	John 14:6
Unspeakable Gift	Sent by God as agent of salvation	2 Corinthians 9:15
Vine	He sustains and nourishes	John 15:5
Way	He is the only road leading to the Father	John 14:5-6

In the space provided, write out John 15:5.

_____

_____

_____

Elaborate on what this verse means to you as a person who is called to impact the world.

_____

_____

_____

Week *One*

To Know Him

Day 5—"God - The Holy Spirit"

Yes, indeed! You have made it to the final run for this week. You are getting more comfortable with the track and the environment around you. The mental prowess for endurance is building as you continue to show up and overcome the hurdles of excuse and limitation. Remember, "Running after God" is not an event, it is a LIFELONG marathon.

Earlier this week, you studied God the Father and God the Son. Today, you will study God – the Holy Spirit.

The Holy Spirit is the third person of the Godhead. The Bible does not give us a personal name for Him as it does for the Father (Elohim, Adonai, etc.) and the Son (Jesus, Messiah, etc). The various appellations (titles) given to Holy Spirit in Scripture simply speak of the office He holds, His work, and the relationship He maintains between God and man regarding the plan of salvation.

He is known as Holy Spirit, Holy Ghost, Spirit of the Lord, Spirit of Christ, Spirit of Truth, and Comforter. He is the part of the Trinity that convicts people of sin and leads them to the Father in repentance and confession. He empowers God's people for witnessing and illuminates their minds to understand His Word. The Holy Spirit is no less God than the Father or the Son. He is completely GOD, the Holy Spirit!

The Holy Spirit is not like Casper the ghost. He is not the wind and contrary to popular opinion, He is not a dove. These things are symbolic of the Holy Spirit, but they are not Him. The Holy Spirit is a person and He has characteristics of personality. Let's look at some of His person-like characteristics.

First Timothy 4:1 says, **"Now the spirit speaketh expressly, that in the latter times some shall depart from the faith, giving heed to seducing spirits, and doctrines of devils."** According to this scripture:

The Holy Spirit

    a. Hears

    b. Speaks

    c. Listens

    d. Prays

Romans 8:26 says, **"Likewise the Spirit also helpeth our infirmities for we know not what we should pray for as we ought: but the Spirit, itself, maketh intercession for us with groanings which cannot be uttered."**

The Holy Spirit

    a. Calls

    b. Convicts

    c. Intercedes

    d. Retaliates

John 15:26 says, **"But when the Comforter is come, whom I will send unto you from the Father, even the Spirit of truth, which proceedeth from the Father, he shall testify of me."**

The Holy Spirit testifies.   True or False

Read John 14:26. Complete the following sentence by unscrambling the word.

The Holy Spirit _____. (hctseea)

Romans 8:14 refers to Holy Spirit as one who _____.

I mentioned earlier that the Holy Spirit is no less God than the Father and the Son. The following scriptures will further clarify that He is God and He possesses all the attributes of God.

He is Omnipresent (everywhere) – Psalm 139:7

He is Omnipotent (all powerful) – Zechariah 4:6

He is Omniscient (all knowing) – Isaiah 40:13

Who is He in Acts 5:4? _____

The work of the Holy Spirit extends throughout the entire Bible. He is mentioned first in Genesis 1:2 and last in Revelation 19:10. Use the following chart as a quick reference tool for some of the name titles given to Holy Spirit. These names reveal important information about Him.

Breath of the Almighty	Job 32:8	Spirit of Christ	Romans 8:9
Comforter	John 14:16	Spirit of Counsel and Might	Isaiah 11:2
Eternal Spirit	Hebrews 9:4	Spirit of Faith	2 Corinthians 4:13
Free Spirit	Isaiah 51:10,12	Spirit of Glory	I Peter 4:14

Good Spirit	Nehemiah 9:20	Spirit of God	Genesis 41:38
Holy Ghost	Acts 20:28	Spirit of Grace	Zechariah 12:10
Holy One	I John 2:20	Spirit of Judgment	Isaiah 4:4
Holy Spirit of God	Ephesians 4:30	Spirit of Knowledge	Isaiah 11:2
Holy Spirit of Promise	Ephesians 1:13	Spirit of Life	Romans 8:2
Power of the Highest	Luke 1:35	Spirit of Prophecy	Revelation 19:10
Seven Spirits	Revelation 4:5	Spirit of Truth	John 14:17
Spirit of Adoption	Romans 8:15	Spirit of Wisdom	Ephesians 1:17

Commit at least one name and scripture to memory. Which one did you choose? _____

Let's end our study today by identifying several symbols of the Holy Spirit. Each symbol has meaning and significance and says something about His nature. This is not an exhaustive list, only a cursory view (quick glance) for the benefit of today's study.

Symbol	Scripture
Dew	Hosea 14:5
Dove	Matthew 3:16
Finger of God	Luke 11:20

Fire	Acts 2:3
Hand of God	2 Chronicles 30:12
Oil	I Samuel 16:13
Seal	Ephesians 1:13
Water	Zechariah 14:8
Wine	Ephesians 5:18

Look at Acts 2:3. In your own words, describe what was going on there.

_____

_____

_____

Read Matthew 3:16. Why do you think the Spirit of God descended like a dove upon Jesus that day? Allow verse 17 to give you a clue. Write your thoughts.

_____

_____

_____

Thank you for running with me this week. I hope that you have benefitted as much as I did. We will continue next week on the track of Intimacy with God. Get some rest and remember to hydrate.

Shalom!

Week 2

GENERAL SESSION

Intimacy with God

"That I may know Him and the power of His resurrection…"
Philippians 3:10, NKJV

GENERAL SESSION
Intimacy with God

Intimacy. This word itself carries a ton of emotions. It takes us right back to what we were studying last week—getting to know God. It's difficult to know someone if you are not intimate with them.

By definition, the word "intimacy" refers to familiarity, of a private nature, personal. This word is akin to a marriage or a strong friendship. When we think in terms of marriage, some of the related words that would clearly help to define intimacy would be words like:

Kinship
Friendship
Fellowship
Devotion
Affection
Intercourse
Commitment
Attachment
Love
Passion
Faithfulness
Fidelity

Intimacy with God comes as we DESIRE to know Him, His plans, His will, and His ways. It is a passionate pursuit. It's not anything that someone can force you to pursue. It is embedded in love and driven by desire!

Listen to what David says in Psalm 27:4:

"One thing I ask of the LORD, this is what I seek; that I may dwell in the house (presence) of the LORD all the days of my life, to gaze upon the beauty of the LORD and to seek him in his temple," (NIV84, emphasis mine).

Do you hear the passion?

Do you sense the affection and commitment towards God?

Look at Psalm 63:1-3:

"O God, you are my God, earnestly, I seek you; my soul thirsts for you, my body longs for you, in a dry and weary land where there is no water. I have seen you in the sanctuary and beheld your power and your glory...your love is better than life" (NIV84).

The Sons of Korah, who were musicians, penned Psalm 42:1-2 (one of my favorite psalms).

"As the deer pants for streams of water, so my soul pants for you, O God. My soul thirsts for God, for the living God. When can I go and meet with God?"

Here's another one. Psalm 84:1-2 was written by David.

"How lovely is your dwelling place (His presence), O LORD Almighty! My soul yearns even faints for the courts of the LORD; my heart and my flesh cry out for the living God" (NIV84, explanation mine).

It's as if being in God's presence and seeking after Him became an addiction for David. He could not get enough of it. Even though

David did some horrible things, He loved God and he went after Him with his whole heart. God even referred to him as a man after His heart. I love this about David, because I too want to seek after Him with all that I have. I want "loving on Him" to be my chief desire.

You are in for an exciting study this week, beginning with defining who you are as God's workmanship (creation, masterpiece). Yes, you were created to do good works that were preordained by God before you made your arrival to planet Earth. So now, if God pre-ordained the works that you should be doing, it only makes sense to seek Him to find out what those works are. Do you really know who you are? What is your God Code?

The week progresses with insights into methods by which we establish intimacy with God: the Word, prayer, praise, and worship.

I love you. Keep running after God; it is the ultimate pursuit.

Shalom!

INDEPENDENT STUDY

Intimacy with God

"That I may know Him and the power of His resurrection…"
Philippians 3:10, NKJV

Week *Two*

Intimacy with God

Day 1—"His Workmanship"

Are you glad to be here my friend? Are you glad for another opportunity to reflect God's glory in the earth? Are you glad for another chance to run after Him with your whole heart? If so, do it! Better yet, let's do it together!

We are changing lanes this week as we focus on "Intimacy with God." In the General Session, we discussed and laid a foundation for this topic. Points of Empowerment included:

Intimacy refers to familiarity, of a private nature, personal.

It is akin to a marriage or strong relationship.

It is a passionate pursuit embedded in love and driven by desire.

Intimacy with God was David's heartbeat as he penned Psalm 63:1-3:

"O God, you are my God, earnestly I seek you; my soul thirsts for you, my body longs for you, in a dry and weary land where there is no water. I have seen you in the sanctuary and beheld your power and glory...your love is better than life" (NIV84).

Today, your focus of study will begin in Ephesians 2:10. The English Standard Version (ESV) reads: **"For we are his workmanship, created in Christ Jesus for good works, which God prepared beforehand, that we should walk in them"** (emphasis mine). The New Living

Translation (NLT) says it this way: **"For we are God's <u>masterpiece</u>. He has created us anew in Christ Jesus, so we can do the good things he planned for us long ago"** (emphasis mine).

Before running after God with your whole heart can become a reality, you will have to know who you are from God's perspective. When you know who you are from His viewpoint, you won't have any image issues or inferiority complexes. Upon His command, you will move forward without question or reservation.

Look at the word "workmanship." According to Webster's Dictionary, "workmanship" means something that was made. In the Greek, the word "workmanship" is translated *poiema*, which means that which is made. The English word "poem" comes from this same Greek word, *poiema*. A poem expresses the thoughts of the poet. It is the heartfelt expression of its author. Do you see the connection?

Think of yourself as being significant to God. Think of your life as being a divinely written poem that expresses the love of God for mankind. Never lose sight of your value. He is counting on you to live in such a way that you help others to see their value and purpose in Him. You are the *poiema* of God. What do you think your life is expressing to others?

_____

_____

_____

Now look at the word "masterpiece," which is another word for workmanship. "Masterpiece" means a person's greatest piece of work. It is a consummate example of skill and excellence. So if we put all of this together to make sense out of the verse, it would sound something like this: "You are God's greatest creation. You were created by Him to do good works that He predestined long ago before you arrived on the earth."

You are an absolute, awesome, authentic creation of God (Jehovah Hoseenu – The Lord our Maker). Psalm 95:6-7 further clarifies this point. It reads: **"O come, let us worship and bow down; let us kneel before the LORD our Maker. For He is our God, and we are the people of His pasture and the sheep of His hand" (NKJV).**

Read Isaiah 64:8 and fill in the blanks.

"But now, O LORD, thou art our father; we are the clay, and thou our potter; and we are the _____ _____ _____ _____."

Because you were made by God, you belong to Him. Because He made you, He knows you. He knows your purpose (universal and individual) and has skillfully designed you to fulfill it. He knows every minute detail about you—your ups, your downs, and your all arounds, He knows! And yes, He knows that you are a work in progress!

Turn in your Bible to Psalm 139. Read verses 1-18. Using the space provided below, summarize this passage in your own words.

_____

_____

_____

_____

In terms of intimacy with God, you were created to worship Him and to bring glory to His name. This includes praise, adoration, thanksgiving, and obedience. Read I Peter 2:9. In your own words, define the phrase "peculiar people." Does it have similar meaning to "workmanship?"

_____

_____

_____

_____

Remember, one of the definitions for workmanship was *poiema*, or poem, in English. I have written a poem for you. I would like for you to add a stanza to your poem. Be prepared to share this in the General Session.

Jehovah's Poem

I am Jehovah's poem, an expression of Him in the earth
Look at me and you will see my beauty and my worth
I am fearfully and wonderfully made, my substance He knows quite well
His masterpiece, His prized possession, a place for Him to dwell
Helping others to see Him is what I love to do
To teach, to pray, and of course, His presence I pursue
I am Jehovah's poem, the rhyme of His story
Spending lots of time with Him and reflecting His glory
This is dedicated to you my friend, you are His poem as well
You are being read by many, and His story you do tell
Jehovah's poem, yes, that's who you are
And it's through YOU He is calling… many from afar!

Write your stanza here:

_____

_____

_____

_____

It's been fun. I like this track! See you tomorrow.

Week *Two*

Intimacy with God

Day 2—"Student of the Word"

Intimacy with God requires spending time in His Word. The Bible has much to say about the Word of God and its' importance to the Believer. As you tighten your shoelaces and focus your gaze, anticipate an increase in your pace today. This will be a quick run with great intensity and impact.

Let's get started in 2 Timothy 2:15.

"Study to shew thyself approved unto God, a workman that needeth not to be ashamed, rightly dividing the word of truth."

The word "study" in this verse means to be diligent. You could read the scripture this way: "Be diligent to show yourself approved unto God…..by rightly dividing the Word of truth."

Does the phrase "rightly dividing the Word of truth" mean that the truth can be wrongly divided? _____ YES _____ NO

Explain your answer: _____

_____

_____

_____

Read 2 Timothy 2:15 from the Amplified Bible and underline the words that mean the same as to "rightly divide."

"Study and be eager and do your utmost to present yourself to God approved (tested by trial), a workman who has no cause to be ashamed, correctly analyzing and accurately dividing [rightly handling and skillfully teaching] the Word of Truth."

The Bible contains the Word of Truth. John 17:17 reads, **"Sanctify them through thy truth: thy word is truth."**

The Word of God should be the foundation upon which we build our lives, families, careers, and everything else that pertains to our experience here in the earth realm. Read Matthew 7:24-25. What will happen to the man whose house (life) is built on a solid foundation? Write your answer below.

_____

_____

_____

_____

You are doing great!

The Word of God is the only source of divine revelation and power that can— and will—sustain you in your walk with God. As you continue to run hard after Him, allow the following scriptures to validate the importance of being a student of the Word. The Word is:

- ❖ Proverb 4:20-22 – medicine and health to our flesh
- ❖ John 20:31 – testimony that Jesus is the Son of God
- ❖ Psalm 119:89 – forever settled in Heaven
- ❖ Romans 1:16 – the power of God

- ❖ Acts 20:29-32 – protection against false teaching
- ❖ Deuteronomy 6:4-9 – necessary for the next generation

Write Psalm 119:105 in the space provided below:

_____

_____

_____

_____

Hosea 4:6 tells us that God's people are destroyed for lack of knowledge, not because knowledge is not available, but because His people reject it. You will not be counted in that number my sister or brother… right? You have embraced the mandate to be a student of the Word. Let's look at some things that could result from living independent of the Word.

1. You would not know Jesus – John 5:46
2. You could not be intimate with God – John 5:19
3. You would not know that you could be healed – Psalm 103:1-3
4. You would lack wisdom – Proverbs 2:6
5. You would not have faith – Romans 10:17
6. You would have no hope – Colossians 1:5
7. You would be defeated and confused – Jeremiah 3:25 and I John 2:14

According to Psalm 119:172, what would be missing in your life if you did not have the Word of God? _____

After studying these scriptures, I am sure you have concluded that life would not be worth living without knowing God and salvation through Jesus Christ, which is found in the Word. Being a student of the Word is paramount to being intimate with God and being a reflection of Him to others.

Take a few minutes and meditate on how knowing God's Word has impacted your life in the last twelve months. I am sure it will cause you to praise Him!

Week *Two*

Intimacy with God

Day 3—"Prayer"

Welcome to day three of the study on Intimacy with God. Today we will talk about a subject that is familiar to all of us. Prayer is one of the basic elements of the believer's life. It is a necessary commodity for true intimacy with the Father.

Prayer is a two-way communication between you and God. In prayer, there is a time when you talk, and a time when you listen. There is a time when God talks, and a time when He listens. If you are doing all the talking all the time and never listening, then you are not engaged in effective prayer (communication with God).

Jesus is the supreme example. As you follow the accounts of His life, you see that He spent an enormous amount of time in prayer. Prayer was His lifeline to the Father. He would get away from the multitudes to spend time communicating with God in prayer (Matthew 14:23).

Read Mark 1:35 then write it in the space provided below.

_____

_____

_____

_____

The Bible provides captivating glimpses into Jesus' prayer life. Let's scroll through a quick list of them. Each will lend itself to applicable prayer practices that could (should) be applied in your life.

- ❖ Jesus' ministry began with prayer – Luke 3:21-22
- ❖ Jesus prayed for others – Matthew 9:13; Luke 22:32
- ❖ Jesus prayed with others – Luke 9:28
- ❖ Jesus prayed alone – Luke 5:16
- ❖ Jesus prayed regularly – Luke 5:16
- ❖ Jesus prayed early in the morning – Mark 1:35
- ❖ Jesus prayed all night (occasionally) – Luke 6:12
- ❖ Jesus prayed with passion – Luke 22:44; Hebrews 5:7
- ❖ Jesus taught the disciples how to pray – Luke 11:1
- ❖ Jesus taught the disciples to pray regularly – Luke 18:1

You can clearly glean from these scriptures that prayer was a lifestyle for Jesus. He was in frequent communication with the Father. The scriptures also reveal that Jesus was never distracted in ministry. He knew the power needed to carry out His assignment would come from God, and God alone. Therefore, He maintained constant, consistent, communication with Him.

What Jesus did, you should do…right? Okay!

Jesus prayed for others. What verse tells you to do the same? Circle your answer.

      a. Revelation 1:1

      b. Psalm 2:1

      c. James 5:16

      d. James 2:12

Jesus prayed passionately. What verse tells you to do the same? Circle your answer.

      a. James 5:16

      b. Job 2:11

      c. Luke 11:7

      d. Psalm 1:1

Jesus prayed regularly. What verse tells you to do the same? Circle your answer.

      a. Luke 7:1

      b. Luke 18:1

      c. Luke 1:18

      d. Luke 17:1

List three things you can do to cultivate a richer prayer life.

_____

_____

_____

_____

There are many types of prayer. Here are a few:

- ❖ Thanksgiving – gratitude
- ❖ Praise and worship – adoration
- ❖ Confession - repentance

- ❖ Petition – supplication (making requests)
- ❖ Meditative – waiting in His presence

Each type of prayer has certain guidelines, which we will discuss in a future lesson. For example, when praying a petition prayer, you should:

- ❖ Ask the Father in Jesus' name – John 16:23
- ❖ Pray the Word of God – I John 5:14
- ❖ Believe you received when you prayed – Mark 11:24
- ❖ Develop a confession of faith – Mark 11:23; Romans 10:10
- ❖ Think and act according to what you believe – I Peter 1:13

To conclude our run for today, write a prayer of thanksgiving in the space provided below.

_____
_____
_____
_____
_____
_____
_____

Week *Two*

Intimacy with God

Day 4—"Praise"

What do you do when you think about the goodness of the Lord? Do you dance? Do you cry? Do you shout? Do you turn yourself about? If I had to guess, I would say you probably do a combination of all the above.

Whether spontaneous or by sacrifice, praise is what you do!

Praise is essential for obtaining and sustaining intimacy with God. It means to express approval, to express adoration of, and to. Praise is a type of prayer. It is a part of worship and it is communication with God.

The book of Psalms is known as the praise book of the Bible. It is inundated with insight on how to praise and why we praise. Psalm 92:1 says **"It is a good thing to give thanks unto the LORD, and to sing praises unto His name, O Most High."** What does Psalm 147:1 tell you about praise?

_____

_____

Match the following references with reasons to praise:

a) Psalm 145:3   _____ Forgives and heals

b) Psalm 136:25   _____ He is great and greatly to be praised

c) Psalm 107:8   _____ He gives food to all flesh

d) Psalm 103:1-3   _____ For His goodness and His wonderful works

e) Psalm 18:46   _____ He is the God of my salvation

Read Psalm 148:1-5 below.

Psalm 148:1-5 **"Praise ye the LORD. Praise ye the LORD from the heavens: praise him in the heights. Praise ye him all his angels: praise ye him all his hosts. Praise ye him sun and moon: praise him all ye stars of light. Praise him, ye heavens of heavens, and ye waters that be above the heavens. Let them praise the name of the LORD: for He commanded, and they were created."**

What is the message of this passage?

    a. Everything in the water should praise God

    b. Everything on the land should praise God

    c. All creation is commanded to praise God

    d. None of the above

Look at the passage above. Underline the sentence that tells you why creation should praise the name of the Lord.

Now let's go a little deeper. There are nine Hebrew words for the English word "praise." The source of this information is derived from *Strong's Exhaustive Concordance of the Bible*.

Hebrew word	Definition	Scripture
Yadah	Extend the hand	Genesis 29:35
Hillool	A celebration of thanksgiving for the harvest	Leviticus 19:24
Tehillah	Laudation; hymn	Deuteronomy 10:21
Barach	To kneel	Judges 5:2
Halal	To celebrate; to boast; to make a show	I Chronicles 16:4
Zamar	To celebrate in music and in song	Psalm 108:1, 21:13
Todah	Adoration, a choir of worshippers	Psalm 42:4, 50:23
Shavach	A loud tone	Psalm 63:3
Shevach	To adore	Daniel 2:23

Praise is a vital part of a life surrendered to God, and it gives credit where credit is due. **"O that men would praise the LORD for his goodness, and for his wonderful works to the children of men!"** (Psalm 107:8).

As we praise God, we rehearse our knowledge of Him, focus on His character and attributes, and come to know Him as who and what we praise Him to be.

In the space provided below, write Psalm 22:3:

___

___

___

Praise will sensitize you to the presence of God. As God inhabits your praises, He downloads information and brings peace, joy, healing, and provision.

You have made it to the end of the fourth lesson for this week, but I have one final request before we call it done. Would you take about three minutes and praise the Lord? Come on! Put your pen and paper down and praise Him. You can sing, dance, shout, or clap your hands. Whatever suits your fancy, just praise Him. He deserves it. Hallelujah!

Week *Two*

Intimacy with God

Day 5—"Worship"

Greetings fellow runner! You have already made it to the end of another week. It appears that time moves faster when you are having fun! The forecast for your run today is favorable. Everything looks great up ahead as you make the final lap for this week.

The spotlight for today is on worship. Worship is a time when we draw near to God (James 4:8). It is a time when we pay deep, sincere, awesome respect, love, and obedience to the One who created us. It is a time of intense focus on the Father for Who He is.

He is Alpha and _____. The _____ and the End (Revelation 22:13).

God wants us to draw near to Him.   True   or   False

James 4:8 tells us if we draw near to God, He will _____

_____

_____

_____

Read John 4:21-24 below.

"Jesus said to her, 'Woman, believe Me, the hour is coming when you will neither on this mountain, nor in <u>Jerusalem</u>, worship the Father. You worship what you do not know; we know what we worship, for <u>salvation is of the Jews</u>. But

the hour is coming, and now is, when the <u>true worshipers</u> will worship the Father in spirit and truth; for the Father is seeking such to worship Him. God is <u>Spirit</u>, and those who worship Him must worship in spirit and truth'" (NKJV, emphasis mine)

Underline the sentence that tells who the Father is seeking to worship Him.

Is that you? _____ Yes_____ No

Now read Matthew 15:7–9 below, then answer the questions that follow.

"Ye hypocrites, well did Esaias prophesy of you saying, this people draweth nigh unto me with their mouth, and honoureth me with their lips; but their heart is far from me. But in vain they do worship me, teaching for doctrines the commandments of men."

Does God accept all worship?_____ Yes_____ No

What did Jesus call those who offered up vain worship?

_____

The purpose of our worship is to glorify, honor, praise, exalt, and please God, not ourselves.   True   or   False

There are five words for Worship in the Greek language:

Greek	Definition	Scripture
Proskuneo	To prostrate oneself; to adore	Matthew 2:2
Sebomahee	To revere	Matthew 15:9
Sebadzomahee	To revere	Romans 1:25
Sebasma	Something adored; an object of worship	2 Thessalonians 2:4
Latryoo-o	To minister to God	Acts 7:42

Moses sings a worship song to the Lord in Exodus 15:1. Write the lyrics to that song in the space provided. (Hint: start after the word "saying.")

_____

_____

_____

Worship is a form of prayer (communicating with God). It requires speaking, listening and doing. As you worship Him today and in the future, remember to spend time listening for His voice. He will give you direction and answers when you wait in His presence.

Read Psalm 16:11. Write the three promises that are available to us in worship.

1. _____
2. _____
3. _____

Great job! You rock!!

Week 3

GENERAL SESSION

Are You in Idolatry

"Thou shalt have no other gods before me."
Exodus 20:3

GENERAL SESSION
Are You in Idolatry

Idolatry is the worship of a physical object as god or immoderate attachment or devotion to something. It is also the worship of false gods or the worship of the true God in a false way. Idolatry is anything that occupies the place that should be occupied by God alone.

One of the most complete definitions of idolatry is found in the book of Exodus, not far from the passages stating the Ten Commandments. Exodus 20:23-24 says, **"Ye shall not make with me gods of silver, neither shall ye make unto you gods of gold."**

The first of the Ten Commandments is:

"Thou shalt have no other gods before me"
Exodus 20:3

Usually when the topic of idolatry comes up, people tend to think of some great statue sitting in front of a shrine in other parts of the world. They may not consider that a television, automobile, addiction, job, or even a political party can be an idol.

A person may not consider that stubbornness, covetousness or selfishness is as idolatry in the eyes of God. Money and success have become modern day idols in the lives of God's people. We must repent and turn from idolatry, because the Scriptures are clear as they warn believers against idols. Idolatry is an abomination to the Lord. It is a dangerous thing. Remember, our God is El Quanna, a jealous God.

Those who make, possess, or worship idols are cursed. To put anything before God or to esteem any created thing more than God—the Creator—is wickedness and a form of idolatry. God's warning is clear:

DO NOT DO IT! What is it about "DO NOT DO IT" that you don't understand? Look at the following scriptures with me:

Exodus 20:3-6: **"Thou shalt have no other gods before me. Thou shalt not make unto thee any graven image, or any likeness of anything that is in heaven above, or that is in the earth beneath, or that is in the water under the earth. Thou shalt not bow down thyself to them, nor serve them: for I the Lord thy God am a jealous God, visiting the iniquity of the fathers upon the children unto the third and fourth generation of them that hate me; And shewing mercy unto thousands of them that love me, and keep my commandments."**

Exodus 20:23: **"Ye shall not make with me gods of silver, neither shall ye make unto you gods of gold."**

What do you interpret this to mean in our generation? Discuss with your group.

_____

_____

_____

Exodus 23:13: **"And in all things that I have said unto you be circumspect: and make no mention of the name of other gods, neither let it be heard out of thy mouth."**

The next verse puts things in perspective. As a matter of fact, it sparks reverential fear. God is a loving Father. He does not want anything bad for you, nor does He want you to get in position to receive the curse. I believe for this reason—and this reason alone—He warns against idolatry. Read Deuteronomy 4:23-24:

"Take heed unto yourselves, lest ye forget the covenant of the LORD your God, which He made with you, and make you a graven image, or the likeness of anything, which the LORD thy God hath forbidden thee. For the LORD thy God is a consuming fire, even a jealous God."

Discuss the meaning of the following phrases with a partner or your small group:

1. Consuming fire
2. Jealous God

Write your notes from the discussion here:

_____

_____

_____

_____

Let's look at the New Testament. It also gives the believer insight and warning against idolatry.

First John 5:20 says, **"And we know that the Son of God is come, and hath given us an understanding, that we may know Him that is true, and we are in Him that is true, even in His Son Jesus Christ. This is the true God, and eternal life. Little children, keep yourselves from idols."**

Complete the following sentence:

Little children, keep _____ from idols.

Is God going to keep you from idols? _____ YES _____ NO

Those that worship idols shall:

- ❖ Perish – Jeremiah 51:18
- ❖ Be cast away – Isaiah 31:7
- ❖ Be ashamed – Isaiah 44:11
- ❖ Be terrified – Isaiah 44:11

None of this is good news. To avoid such tragedies will require obedience on your part. DO NOT IGNORE THE WARNING SIGNS!

Here is your homework. Ask the Holy Spirit to reveal to you any idol you may have established in your life. When He does, get rid of it.

As a group, discuss and list three (3) things that could easily become idols in our culture. Example: technology (cell phones, videos, iPads).

_____

_____

_____

_____

INDEPENDENT STUDY

Are You in Idolatry

"Thou shalt have no other gods before me."
Exodus 20:3

Week *Three*

Are You in Idolatry

Day 1—"A Jealous God"

Happy Third Week! You are progressing quite well as we continue our study on *Running after God, The Ultimate Pursuit.* You are at the halfway mark, and I know you are not considering turning around now. You have been a great companion and an excellent pacesetter! Come on, take a deep breath in and blow it out. Do it again—breathe in, breathe out. Let's go!

The General Session was sobering as you dealt with the topic of idolatry. It was thought provoking in that it highlighted the fact that God does not take idolatry lightly. The sin of idolatry was an offense to the glory of God. The Israelites, whom God had saved and shown His mercy to, forgot about what God had done for them and started worshipping a calf (Psalm 106:19-21). Reflect back to your notes from the General Session and complete the following:

Write the first commandment in the space provided below (Exodus 20:3).

_____

_____

_____

_____

Exodus 20:23-24: **"Ye shall not make with me gods of _____, neither shall ye make unto you gods of _____."**

The question is, "Why shouldn't you do those things?" Look in Exodus 20:5. Write your answer.

_____

_____

_____

_____

You are correct! He (our God) is a jealous God (El Qanna).

Write Exodus 34:14.

_____

_____

_____

_____

Tell the truth. When you hear the word "jealousy," what do you think about? Do you immediately think of a husband who does not allow his wife to leave the house without him, because he thinks she is going to see another man? Maybe your first thought was of a nagging, suspicious wife who is always accusing her husband of cheating. Better yet, maybe you thought of a girlfriend who is always spying on her boyfriend.

Is jealousy a bad word? In the story *Othello*, Shakespeare referred to jealousy as the "green-eyed monster." Today, jealousy has overtones of selfishness and distrust. It implies hostility toward others. It is possessive in nature, demanding and overbearing. It destroys trust, awakens fear, and tears down self-esteem. It is responsible for countless divorces, broken dreams, derailed destinies, and premature deaths.

How can God be jealous? The Bible says He is love. The Bible says He is kind. The Bible says God is holy.

Webster's Dictionary gives the following definitions for the word "jealousy:"

1. apprehensive of loss of exclusive devotion
2. intolerance of rivalry or unfaithfulness
3. hostile toward one believed to enjoy an advantage
4. vigilant to guard a possession

In your opinion, which one of these definitions would you choose as the best fit to describe the jealousy God has for His children?

_____

_____

Zelos is the Greek word for jealousy. It means zeal. In fact, both the Old and New Testament words for jealousy are translated as zeal. Being jealous and being zealous are essentially the same in the Bible. According to Richard Strauss, the root idea in the Old Testament word "jealous" is to become intensely red. It was associated with the rising heat of emotions, which are, in turn, associated with zeal. God is zealous about protecting what belongs to Him.

What scripture did you study last week that supports the statement, "You belong to God?" (Ephesians)

_____

_____

_____

_____

Complete the following verse. Psalm 135:4:

"For the LORD has chosen Jacob for Himself, _____

_____

_____

Using Psalm 78:58, how did God's people provoke Him to jealousy?

    a. with their high places

    b. graven images

    c. a only

    d. a and b

Explain what God was not willing to give to anyone in Isaiah 42:8?

_____

_____

_____

_____

When thinking of God's jealousy, remember the opening words of John 3:16: For God so loved you…

See you tomorrow!

Week *Three*

Are You in Idolatry

Day 2—"Disobedience"

You have to dig from within this week as we continue to study the not-so- popular topic of idolatry. In order for you to run after God with all of your heart, you will have to address the issues that might stand as obstacles in your way. Disobedience is one such issue.

Before you explore disobedience, let's journey through the streets of its antithesis, obedience. I believe if you know what it means to be obedient, a clearer understanding of disobedience will emerge.

Obedience is defined as practically accepting the will of God as authority. It goes beyond just saying it. It becomes an outward expression in your life. You become a DOER of the Word and not just a HEARER of the Word (James 1:22). Obedience to God means you are in agreement with Him. Your modus operandi becomes, "Whatever God says, I will do."

Let's pull in some scripture for support. Read Deuteronomy 11:26-28 below.

> *"See, I am setting before you today a blessing and a curse — the blessing if you obey the commands of the LORD your God that I am giving you today; the curse if you disobey the commands of the LORD your God and turn from the way that I command you today by following other gods, which you have not known"* (NIV84).

What do you receive if you obey the commands (Word) of the Lord?

_____

_____

_____

Read 1 Samuel 15:22-23. Underline the sentence that snatches your attention regarding obedience to God.

"But Samuel replied: Does the LORD delight in burnt offerings and sacrifices as much as in obeying the voice of the LORD? To obey is better than sacrifice, and to heed is better than the fat of rams. For rebellion is like the sin of divination, and arrogance like the evil of idolatry. Because you have rejected the word of the LORD, he has rejected you as king" (NIV84).

Read John 14:15, 21 and complete the following sentence.

You love Jesus, therefore you will _____.

What can you infer from the above scriptures?

      a. God expects us to obey Him

      b. God is not concerned either way

      c. None of the above

      d. All of the above

So now, what is disobedience? It's the opposite of obedience, right? Before you refer to the dictionary, write your definition for disobedience below.

_____

_____

_____

_____

I love smart students and you are truly one of them!

To be disobedient is to yield to your own will and not the will of God. To be disobedient is to follow after other gods (self, money, and career). Disobedience is any choice that is contrary to what God has instructed.

You must understand that disobedience and idolatry are partners, they co-exist. Both are derivatives of pride and rebellion. Refer back to 1 Samuel 15:22-23 above. Circle the words that are connected to disobedience.

Write Deuteronomy 28:14.

_____

_____

_____

_____

You have read enough scripture to know that disobedience has consequences. Answer the following:

When Adam sinned in the Garden, what was the consequence (Genesis 3:17)?

_____

_____

_____

_____

When Jonah disobeyed God, what did it cost him (Jonah 1:1-5)?

_____

_____

_____

_____

In Numbers 20:8,12, God told Moses to "speak to the rock." Instead, he hit the rock with his rod. What was the devastating consequence for Moses' disobedience?

_____

_____

_____

_____

God commands us to love one another. Do you think there is a consequence for disobeying God on this issue? _____ YES _____ NO

If you have been in disobedience in any way, it is not too late to put an end to it. First John 1:9 states, **"If we confess our sins, he is faithful and just to forgive us our sins and to cleanse us from all unrighteousness."** Don't hesitate, my sisters and brothers. Confess and be cleansed. Go and sin no more. Jesus loves you!

Read Psalm 51:1-19. Summarize in your own words:

_____

_____

_____

_____

Shalom!

Week Three

Are You in Idolatry

Day 3—"Identifying the Idols"

First John 2:15-16 says, **"Do not love the world or anything in the world. If anyone loves the world, the love of the Father is not in him. For everything in the world—the cravings of sinful man, the lust of his eyes and the boasting of what he has and does—comes not from the Father but from the world"** (NIV84).

The Message Bible says it this way:

"Don't love the world's ways. Don't love the world's goods. Love of the world squeezes out love for the Father. Practically everything that goes on in the world—wanting your own way, wanting everything for yourself, wanting to appear important—has nothing to do with the Father. It just isolates you from Him."

That will shake your cage right there!

Hello my friend, it's an uphill run today. It's steep and demanding, but you can do it! Steep, because this is a path not frequently traveled (a high place), and demanding, because it will cause you to examine yourself to identify any idols you may have erected in your life.

This lesson reminds me of a workout that I did with a friend yesterday. We are both over 55 years old and very excited about being able to move…especially to run and walk for almost two hours non-stop. During our session, my friend had the idea to run the hills after we had completed our first hour. Our minds wanted to, but we had to MAKE our bodies cooperate. That is what you will have to do regarding this lesson. You will have to mentally conceive what the Holy Spirit is revealing today and then, MAKE yourself obey. This lesson is designed to expose idolatry at a personal level.

To get started, let's review a definition of idolatry.

Idolatry, in Christian theology, is "the worship of a created object" rather than the true God. The term "idol" often refers to conceptual constructs such as fame, money, nationality, ethnicity, and the ritual of attachment related to these is considered idolatry.

Anything that is more important than obeying God could be considered an idol. It's not that you blatantly disobey God—you are going to do it eventually, but not right now. There is something else more important that you need to accomplish and then, you will do what God said. Do not feel like the lone ranger here. God has corrected me many times about this very thing. Read and write Matthew 6:21 in the space below.

_____

_____

_____

_____

Now read Joel 2:12-13 in the New Living Translation.

"That is why the LORD says, 'Turn to me now, while there is time. Give me your hearts. Come with fasting, weeping, and mourning. Don't tear your clothing in your grief, but tear your hearts instead.' Return to the LORD your God, for He

is merciful and compassionate, slow to get angry and filled with unfailing love. He is eager to relent and not punish."

What does God want from you?

    a. your treasure

    b. your heart

    c. your time

    d. none of the above

God wants your heart because everything you do will follow your heart. Proverbs 4:23 instructs us to keep (protect) our heart with all diligence; for out of it are the issues of life.

In an effort to help you identify any idols that you may have in your life, answer the following questions:

What has most of your attention and affection?

_____

_____

_____

Are you afraid to lose this person or thing?	__ YES __ NO
Does it demand most of your time/thoughts?	__ YES __ NO
Does this person or thing give you a sense of worth?	__ YES __ NO
Do you invest most of your money in this person or thing?	__ YES __ NO
Does it cause you to disobey God repeatedly?	__ YES __ NO
Does your protection of it cause conflict in your life?	__ YES __ NO
Has the Holy Spirit warned you about it?	__ YES __ NO

Sadly my friend, you may be in idolatry. I know it is not your intent but nevertheless, if it fits the protocol above, it is an idol. For further clarification, read Jeremiah 1:16-3:20. These scriptures will reveal how seriously God views idols in our lives. You will discover that He compares idolatry to adultery in our relationship with Him. Here is an excerpt of a few verses from that passage.

Jeremiah 2:7-8, 11-12, 20 (NLT):

"And when I brought you into a fruitful land to enjoy its bounty and goodness, you defiled my land and corrupted the possession I had promised you. The priests did not ask, 'Where is the LORD?' Those who taught my word ignored me, the rulers turned against me, and the prophets spoke in the name of Baal, wasting their time on worthless idols... Has any nation ever traded its gods for new ones, even though they are not gods at all? Yet my people have exchanged their glorious God for worthless idols!... On every hill and under every green tree, you have prostituted yourselves by bowing down to idols."

Jeremiah 3:2-3 (NLT)

"Look at the shrines on every hilltop. Is there any place you have not been defiled by your adultery with other gods? You sit like a prostitute beside the road waiting for a customer. You sit alone like a nomad in the desert. You have polluted the land with your prostitution and your wickedness. That's why even the spring rains have failed. For you are a brazen prostitute and completely shameless."

Modern idolatry has one thing as its central core—self. God's people no longer bow down to golden calves, instead, we worship the god of SELF. You know the cliché, "It's all about me."

Some examples? I'm glad you asked!

Power	Pastors
Possessions	Tradition
Influence	Hobbies
Children	Family
Ministry	Success
People	Career

How can a hobby become an idol?

_____

_____

_____

How can a pastor become an idol?

_____

_____

_____

How can your possessions become an idol?

_____

_____

_____

Pray this prayer with me:

Father, in the name of Jesus, I confess that I have committed the sin of idolatry, which is putting other things (gods) before You. I ask You to forgive me and to cleanse me from this unrighteousness. I ask You to reveal anything else that I have put in the wrong place and help me to stop it. Help me to leave it. Help me to put it down. It is my desire to please You with my life, because You are the only true and living God. As David prayed, I pray, create in me a clean heart and renew the right spirit within me, in the name of Jesus. Amen.

Week *Three*

Are You in Idolatry

Day 4—"Getting Rid of Idols"

This is a short run today, still steep, but not as long. Now that you have identified the idols in your life, you will begin the process of getting rid of them—once and for all!

Let's go to the Word of God in I John 1:8-10. Complete the following sentences.

"If we say we have no sin, we deceive _____.

If we confess our _____, he is _____ and just to _____ us our sins, and to _____ us from all unrighteousness.

If we say that we have not sinned, we make him a liar, and his _____ is not in us."

God loves you so much, no matter what you have done or what may be going on in your life, He always provides an escape route. First Corinthians 10:13 reveals this truth. Read it and answer the following question.

In your own words, explain the phrase "a way of escape."

_____
_____
_____

There is another phrase that illuminates when you read this verse. Write that phrase below.

"…but _____ _____ faithful…"

Did you know that God was referring to idolatry in this scripture? _____YES _____ NO

Write 1 Corinthians 10:14 in the space below:

_____

_____

_____

Put the pedal to the metal!

Here is the message so far on getting rid of idols.

1. Confess your sins
2. God will forgive you
3. He is faithful
4. He will provide the way of escape
5. Flee idolatry
6. Here is the success formula for getting rid of idols:

Code: AQG – 123

Admit – Confession – I John 1:9

Quit – Repentance – II Chronicles 7:14

Get Fit – Exercise your faith – Mark 11:23-24

1. Read/Hear the Word – 2 Timothy 3:16-17
2. Pray often – Luke 18:1
3. Surrender to God – Romans 12:1-2; I Corinthians 6:19

In some severe cases, individuals may have to go through deliverance, get healing from soul ties, follow a written restoration plan, and establish a safety net of accountability. If you fit into this category, do what you need to do. Bottom line, get rid of the idols.

Praise the Lord!

Week *Three*

Are You in Idolatry

Day 5—"Focus on God (F.O.G.)"

Okay my friend, I need to add something to our lesson from yesterday before we move forward. You were given some tips regarding getting rid of the idols in your life. If your idol is your family—whether it's your spouse, children, sister or brother—you cannot get rid of them. You must ask God to help you to not idolize them. Repent for the sin of idolatry and continue to love the person. They are not God and would be a lousy substitute for Him. This includes other people as well, such as your pastor or your boss. Praise the Lord? Amen.

You have made it over the wall and gotten the "monkey" off your back. Your steps are in cadence with a comfortable pace that will take you to the finish line for this week. Your run will not be hard, yet it will require focus.

I had a dream last week that I was driving a truck down the street. Actually, it appeared to be in California where the streets wind around the mountains. I was driving very comfortably, leaning back in the seat. It was extremely foggy, but that did not concern me because I knew God was with me. I was so comfortable that I was not even focusing on the street; I was just driving! Then I heard the voice of God. He said, "Sit up, pay attention, and keep your focus on Me." I began to look around, but the fog was so dense that I still could not see. Then all of a sudden, I began to see the letters "F.O.G." With the help of the Holy Spirit, I knew those letters were an acronym for "Focus on God."

Even though, in the natural, you may be in fog and things may seem discombobulated and unclear right now, God's message to you today is to keep your focus. Get into the supernatural F.O.G. He will bring you successfully through your current situation. Hallelujah!

Your focus today will include "re-throning" the Most High in your life. This means that you will allow God to rule in your situations. You will handle every issue in a manner that pleases Him. His Word will be your final authority, and it will settle any argument that rises against you.

Idolatry is a stronghold that must be dealt with. It must be bound and the supply sources must be cut off. It is a stronghold that will pass down to other generations, if left unattended (Jeremiah 5:7-19; Ezekiel 8:6-8).

Here is a great place to focus to fine tune your view. Read 2 Corinthians 10:4-5 and write it below.

_____

_____

_____

Great! Now, you are beginning to put God where He should be in your life. He is greater than any problem that faces you.

Second Corinthians 10:4 talks about weapons of warfare. Explain.

_____

_____

_____

Wonderful!

Let's take a closer look at some of the weapons you have in your spiritual arsenal. As you F.O.G., you'll discover that you are not at a disadvantage when it comes to idolatry. God has given you authority (power) over all the ability of the devil and nothing shall by any means hurt you (or prevent you from moving forward in life (Luke 10:18-19).

Weapon #1 – The Word of God

Psalm 119:11 says, **"Thy word have I hid in mine heart, that I might not sin against thee."**

Psalm 119:105 says, **"Thy word is a lamp unto my feet, and a light unto my path."**

Write Hebrews 4:12:

_____

_____

_____

Weapon #2 – Fasting

Matthew 17:21 says, **"Howbeit this kind goeth not out but by prayer and fasting."**

Matthew 6:16 says, **"Moreover when ye fast, be not, as the hypocrites, of a sad countenance."**

Write Luke 2:37:

_____

_____

Weapon # 3 – Prayer

Luke 18:1 says, **"And he spake a parable unto them to this end, that men ought always to pray, and not to faint."**

James 5:16 says, **"Confess your faults one to another, and pray one for another, that ye may be healed. The effectual fervent prayer of a righteous man availeth much."**

Write Isaiah 65:24:

_____

_____

_____

Weapon #4 – Love

John 3:16 says, **"For God so loved the world, that he gave his only begotten Son, that whosoever believeth in him should not perish, but have everlasting life."**

First John 4:16 says, **"And we have known and believed the love that God hath to us. God is love; and he that dwelleth in love dwelleth in God, and God in him."**

Write I John 4:18:

_____

_____

_____

Weapon #5 – Faith

Hebrews 11:1 says, **"Now faith is the substance of things hoped for, the evidence of things not seen."**

Hebrews 11:6 says, **"But without faith it is impossible to please him: for he that cometh to God must believe that he is, and that he is a rewarder of them that diligently seek him."**

Write 2 Corinthians 5:7:

_____

_____

_____

Deploy your weapons! Activate them daily!

F.O.G. - Focus on God. Fine tune your view and He will keep you in perfect peace, in a place of security and victory over idolatry (Isaiah 26:23).

It's been a rewarding week.

Shalom!

Week 4
GENERAL SESSION

Divine Treasure Hunt

"And ye shall seek me, and find me, when ye shall search for me with all your heart."
Jeremiah 29:13

GENERAL SESSION
Divine Treasure Hunt

Let's start by looking at a few foundational scriptures.

Matthew 6:33 says, **"But seek ye first the kingdom of God, and His righteousness, and, these things shall be added unto you."**

Hebrews 11:6 says, **"Without faith it is impossible to please him, for he that cometh to God must believe that he is, and that he is a rewarder of them that diligently seek Him."**

Matthew 16:24-25 says, **"Then said Jesus unto his disciples, if any man will come after me, let him deny himself, and take up his cross, and follow me. For whosoever will save his life shall lose it; and whosoever will lose his life for my sake shall find it."**

Let's peruse through each of these scriptures. What illuminates in my mind when I read Matthew 6:33 is the word "first." You must put God first! And when you do, everything else is taken care of.

In Hebrews 11:6, two words snatch my attention: "rewarder" and "diligently." God blesses you when you obey and seek Him. You must also be diligent about it. The word "diligent" means to do something with perseverance, painstaking effort, steady application…you are always on your job! Those are the type of people who get great rewards.

In Matthew 16:24-25, three phrases stand out: "First let him deny himself" – don't seek to have your own way, it's not all about you—your plans have to take a back seat to God's will for you. Second "take up his cross" – this is a good one because most of us read right past it. Everyday you must take up your cross. This means that anything that Jesus bore on the cross as a substitute for you, you must stand against it. You must obey God's Word, even when your flesh does not agree. Lastly, "follow me" – imitate Jesus, do what He did, obey, pray, love, forgive, and speak not a word when people say crazy things about you. Hallelujah!

God wants you to seek Him without excuse and with a sense of urgency. He wants you to have a sense that if I don't get with God, I am not going to make it.

Look at Psalm 42:1-2

"As the hart panteth after the water brooks, so panteth my soul after thee, O God…My soul thirsteth for God, for the living God."

This deer was not out prancing and dancing. He was at the point of exhaustion. He had been preyed upon by predators and had become thirsty, maybe to the point of dehydration. He desperately needed water to survive. David uses this deer as an object of reference while praying to God. He said (I paraphrase) "Lord, just like the deer needs the water to live, I need You. I thirst for You. It's tough out here without You. You are my lifeline." God was there for David and because He is no respector of persons, He is there for you. He knows what you are going through. He is more sensitive to where you are than anything or anyone else. Look at Psalm 42:7. It says that deep calleth unto deep!

Get with your partner/group. Read and discuss Deuteronomy. 4:29. Write your discussion notes in the space below:

_____

_____

_____

Hosea 10:12 tells us to break up the fallow ground; for it is time to seek the Lord. Seeking God produces great rewards. What does it produce in the following passages?

1. Psalm 70:4 _____
2. 2 Chronicles 14:7 _____
3. Jeremiah 33:3 _____
4. Proverbs 28:5 _____
5. Isaiah 40:31 _____
6. Matthew 6:33 _____
7. Psalm 27:4-5 _____

Get ready! This is going to be a powerful week.

INDEPENDENT STUDY

Divine Treasure Hunt

"And ye shall seek me, and find me, when ye shall search for me with all your heart."
Jeremiah 29:13

Week *Four*

Divine Treasure Hunt

Day 1—"Wisdom"

Hello, and welcome to week four of your study in *Running after God, The Ultimate Pursuit*. This week, you will participate in a Divine Treasure Hunt. For the next five days, you will enjoy your run as it takes you through lush green meadows with beautiful flowers and flowing waterfalls. With a forecast to live for: sunshine, clear skies, light winds, and 76° Fahrenheit. Gorgeous! It's the perfect backdrop from which to set your pace for today.

Your path will encompass the book of Proverbs, specifically. You will glean from the wisdom of Solomon as he so eloquently gives you tools you can use, to be all God has called you to be and do all He has called you to do.

In running after God, there are some things that you must know and do. If you recall, your session from last week ended with highlighting a number of spiritual weapons that you possess as a believer. Today you will enhance your arsenal of weaponry as we discuss wisdom and its role in pursuing God.

Read Proverbs 4:7. Write what it says.

_____

_____

_____

If I would ask you to write a definition for wisdom, you would probably go to the dictionary for assistance. But let's embrace a paradigm shift right here. Read Job 28:12-13. According to this scripture, can man—of his own intellect—give a true definition of wisdom? _____YES _____ NO

The true definition of wisdom is found in Job 28:23, 28. Read it below.

"God understandeth the way thereof, and He knoweth the place thereof. And unto man he said, Behold, the fear of the LORD, that is wisdom; and to depart from evil is understanding."

What is wisdom?

_____

_____

_____

Where would you find the following scripture?

"The fear of the LORD is the beginning of wisdom, and the knowledge of the Holy One is understanding" (NKJV).

    a. Proverbs 1:2

    b. Proverbs 9:12

    c. Proverbs 9:10

    d. None of the above

It is important to make this insertion before we go deeper into this, because even though Solomon wrote Proverbs, **God** is actually speaking to you through him. As you continue to conquer this terrain, allow God to download precious nuggets for your treasure box. It is truly a DIVINE hunt.

It is equally important to indicate that this lesson is specifically focusing on godly wisdom, and not the wisdom of man.

Look at Proverbs 2:1- 8. There are several action verbs expressed throughout this passage. As you read the passage, underline those words that tell you to do something.

> *"My son, if thou wilt receive my words, and hide my commandments with thee; So that thou incline thine ear unto wisdom, and apply thine heart to understanding; Yea, if thou criest after knowledge, and liftest up thy voice for understanding; If thou seekest her as silver, and searchest for her as for hid treasures; Then shalt thou understand the fear of the LORD, and find the knowledge of God. For the LORD giveth wisdom: out of his mouth cometh knowledge and understanding. He layeth up sound wisdom for the righteous: he is a buckler to them that walk uprightly. He keepeth the paths of judgment, and preserveth the way of his saints."*

Let's look closer at the words you underlined:

- ❖ Receive
- ❖ Hide
- ❖ Incline
- ❖ Apply
- ❖ Criest
- ❖ Liftest
- ❖ Seek
- ❖ Search

Words	Definitions
Receive	To take into one's possession; to act as a receptacle or container
Hide	To hoard or reserve; to protect
Incline	To prick up the ears; strain to hear, hearken, give heed, mark well
Apply	To stretch or spread out; cause to yield
Criest	Call out to; i.e. properly, address by name
Liftest	Give with greatest latitude of application; call aloud
Seek	Search out (specifically in worship and prayer); strive after
Search	Seek causatively; diligent

As it relates to treasure, this passage is a gold mine! It holds within it profound messages regarding wisdom. One such message is that in order for you to have godly wisdom, you will have to be a container of the Word of God and protect the Word that is in you. It goes on to say that in pursuing the Word, you must sometimes "strain to hear it." In other words, with all the noise (issues) that is going on around you, you will have to make time for the Word of God. You must call aloud and be diligent to search it out through prayer, praise and worship.

Is this similar to the message you received from this passage?

__YES __ NO

Explain:

_____

_____

_____

In verse 4, the phrase "for hid treasures" is referring to:

    a, Wisdom

    b. Love

    c. Worship

    d. Praise

Read verse 5 of this passage. The definition for "wisdom" is embedded therein. Underline that definition.

"Then, shalt thou understand the fear of the LORD, and find the knowledge of God."

What is the fear of the Lord? _____

To reiterate, wisdom is paramount in your pursuit after God. You have discovered that it is a hidden treasure. To bring our run to a successful end today, which of the following best describes wisdom?

    a. A secret

    b. A secreted valuable buried

    c. An unknown treasure

    d. None of the above

Shalom!

Week *Four*

Divine Treasure Hunt

Day 2—"Wisdom"

Today is going to be a sprint. You will continue the lesson from yesterday and close out Proverbs 2:1-8. The foundational scripture from yesterday,

Proverbs 4:7, supported our purpose for highlighting wisdom as a part of the Divine Treasure Hunt.

Proverbs 4:7:

"Wisdom is the principal thing; therefore get wisdom: and with all thy getting get understanding."

You accented certain action words that led to the acquisition of the fear of the Lord and knowledge of God. Those words included: receive, hide, ____, _____, criest, liftest, _____, _____.

That's the way to do it! Thumbs up!

I want you to move down to verse 6 of Proverbs chapter 2. In verses 1-4, God was telling you to do certain things to discover the treasure in verse 5. Now notice the Lord begins to take action in verse 6.

Write Proverbs 2:6 in the space provided below:

_____

_____

_____

The Lord giveth what? _____

Out of His mouth cometh _____ and _____.

Read Isaiah 55:8-13 and explain the importance of having godly wisdom.

_____

_____

_____

Go back to Proverbs chapter 2 and read verse 7. **"He layeth up (stores up) sound wisdom for the righteous…"**

Read 2 Corinthians 5:21.

Who is the righteous? _____. (Hint: a two letter word beginning with "m.")

Proverbs 2:8 says, **"He keepeth the paths of judgement, and preserveth the way of his saints."**

The phrase: **"preserveth the way of his saints,"** means that God guards, protects, and attends to the course of life of His children.

Do you feel that God has been guarding you and protecting your path? If yes, give an example. If no, please explain.

_____ YES _____ NO

_____

_____

_____

You will end your sprint for today as we look at verse 9. **"Then shalt thou understand righteousness, and judgment and equity; yea, every good path."** In summary, when you get godly wisdom, you will know what is right, just and fair—and you will know what to do in every situation.

Perfect!

Week *Four*

Divine Treasure Hunt

Day 3—"Pearls of Great Price"

A good run is the order for this day. I trust that you are still on track, keeping moderate pace as you progress through the lush green meadows of the Divine Treasure Hunt. The view has been captivating indeed, as you looked at the valuable treasure of wisdom. Today, you will set your gaze upon treasure that is hid in the field. Get your Bible and open it to Matthew 13:44-46 and let's take a look at it together. Ready! Set! Read!

> *"Again, the kingdom of heaven is like unto treasure hid in a field; the which when a man hath found, he hideth, and for joy thereof goeth and selleth all that he hath, and buyeth that field. Again, the kingdom of heaven is like unto a merchant man, seeking goodly pearls: Who, when he had found one pearl of great price, went and sold all that he had, and bought it."*

Underline the phrases "treasure hid in a field" and "pearl of great price" in the passage above. Circle the word "man" and place a box around the word "field" in the passage.

In Matthew the thirteenth chapter, Jesus is speaking to the multitudes in several parables. Verse 35 tells us Jesus was speaking secrets that had been kept from the foundation of the world. Jesus explained the meaning of one of the parables in verses 37-43. Read these verses and answer the following questions:

1. Who is the sower that sows good seed?

    a. Son of David

    b. Seed of Abraham

    c. Son of Man

    d. Satan

2. Who is the Son of Man?

    a. Jesus

    b. Believers

    c. Satan

    d. None of the above

3. The field represents the

    a. Kingdom

    b. World

    c. Body

    d. All of the above

4. The pearl is something of great

    a. Beauty

    b. Price

    c. Waste

    d. Deception

You are making much progress my friend! It's a short distance run today so you are almost there. Let's continue.

In verse 44, Jesus makes reference to "treasure hid in the field." You already know that the field represents the world. Well, what is the treasure that is hid in the world? The word "treasure" is being used metaphorically and symbolizes something other than jewels that you would put in a jewelry box.

Read Exodus 19:5-6:

"Now therefore, if ye will obey my voice indeed, and keep my covenant, then ye shall be a peculiar treasure unto me above all people: for all the earth is mine: And ye shall be unto me a kingdom of priests, and an holy nation. These are the words which thou shalt speak unto the children of Israel."

Read Psalm 135:4 and write it in the space below.

_____

_____

_____

Who specifically is God calling His treasure? _____

You are absolutely correct; God is referring to Israel. From previous studies, we know that prophetically Israel refers to God's people—the Church—you and me. Amen? Now read Malachi 3:16-17 for additional support.

You are the treasure that is hid in the world. Yes, YOU are the "pearl of great price." Isn't that exciting? The word "hid" simply refers to protected. Though you are in the world, you are not of the world. You are hidden in Christ Jesus.

Read John 17:16:

"They are not of the world, even as I am not of the world."

Read Colossians 3:3

"For ye are dead, and your life is hid with Christ in God."

As you look at these scriptures, you realize that at one time, you were also in the world, but by and through grace, you were saved. Here's the power point: In the world, there are others who are potential "pearls of great price." They too can become "treasures hid in the field." As a person who is running after God, what do you think you can do to add to the treasure chest of the Kingdom of God? In the space below, tell what you can do and how you will do it.

_____

_____

_____

_____

_____

_____

See you tomorrow!

Week *Four*

Divine Treasure Hunt

Day 4—"Potential Pearls"

Yesterday, you read in Matthew 13:44 where the treasure (God's people) is hid in the field (the world). Today, I want to direct your attention to Matthew 13:24-30 where it talks about a man who sowed good seed into the field but as he slept, the enemy came and sowed tares (weeds) among the wheat. The servant came and asked if he should pull up the tares. Look at what Jesus says in verse 29. Write it below:

_____

_____

_____

Who do you think the wheat represents?

    a. The believer

    b. The unbeliever

    c. Jesus

    d. God

If the wheat represents the believer, then who does the tare represent?

    a. The believer

    b. The unbeliever

    c. Jesus

    d. God

Awesome!

Verse 29 of Matthew 13 gives you some insight as to where these two groups of people are located and the proximity of the space between them.

What would you say?
Are they in close proximity? _____ YES _____ NO

How do you know that? (Hint: see verse 29.)

_____

_____

_____

According to verse 30, the wheat and the tares will grow together until harvest. The word "harvest" means the time for gathering the mature crops from the field.

What will happen to the tares?

_____

_____

_____

What will happen to the wheat?

_____

_____

_____

If the tares represent the unbeliever, that person will be lost forever. Is that God's will? _____ YES _____ NO

Write 2 Peter 3:9 in the space below:

_____

_____

_____

Let's go back to Matthew 13:45-46. It reads:

"Again, the kingdom of heaven is like unto a merchant man (Jesus), seeking goodly pearls: Who, when he had found a pearl of great price, went and sold all that He had, and bought it" (explanation mine).

Jesus came to seek and save those who were lost (Luke 19:10). I believe you and I are hidden treasure and pearls of great price. I further believe that we are surrounded by potential hidden treasure and pearls of great price, and these pearls are waiting for the laborers (you and me) to show up to harvest them.

First Corinthians 7:23 reveals that we were bought with a price. That price was the precious blood of Jesus. Read I Peter 1:18-19 and fill in the blanks:

"Forasmuch as ye know that ye were not redeemed with corruptible things, as silver and gold, from your vain conversation received by tradition from your fathers; But with the _____ _____ _____, **as a lamb without blemish and without spot."**

At this point, I am reminded of another scripture in Matthew 6:19-20 which tells you to "lay not up for yourselves treasures upon the earth…but instead, lay up for yourselves treasures in heaven" (paraphrased).

I want you to consider this thought. The only thing you can take to heaven with you is people. You can't take money. There is no money in heaven. You can't take your car. They are not driving cars down the streets of gold. You can't take your house. You already have a mansion waiting for you.

So what can you take? Treasure! That potential treasure and pearl of great price is in the field (world) right around you. They are called *sinners* now, but as you look into the field, you will see that they are ripe for harvesting. Go get them!

Enjoy your treasure hunt!

Week *Four*

Divine Treasure Hunt

Day 5—"Grace"

Whew, this has been a time of reckoning! Continue your scenic run on to the finish line for this week. You have run the track of wisdom, pearls of great price and potential pearls of great price. Today, you will run the track of grace. Grace is a priceless treasure. As a matter of fact, you can't purchase it. You can't work for it. It is the gift of God. Let's warm up and get started.

Read Ephesians 2:8-9:

"For by grace are ye saved through faith; and that not of yourselves: it is the gift of God: Not of works, lest any man should boast."

The word "grace" comes from a Greek word *charis*, which means favor.

This is going to be one lap around the track, a short run with long impact! I had planned for this lesson to go in another direction. This was not the original plan. The original plan stopped with the General Session. Nevertheless, let God's will be done.

You are a person after God's heart. You are running after Him and because of that, He wants you to know some things. First, you will need wisdom for the journey. Second, you need the correct perspective of yourself—you are a pearl of great price. Third, you need to know that you cannot be satisfied with the fact that you know Him—you must bring others with you, for they are potential pearls of great price.

And lastly, you must know that the pursuit of running after Him can only take place by His grace. It's not because of your works, where you live, or where you go to church—but it is only because of God's grace. Grace is a divine treasure.

I would like to share several Grace Nuggets with you as we bring this lesson, "Divine Treasure Hunt," to a close for this week.

Without grace, salvation would be impossible (Ephesians 2:8-9).

God's grace is sufficient for you. You have enough grace to overcome any— and everything the world or the devil throws at you. Go on and confess: God's grace is sufficient for me. I can and I will overcome! (2 Corinthians 12:9).

You were separated from your mother's womb and called by grace. Man did not call you. You were called by _____ (Galatians 1:15).

You are justified by grace

Titus 3:7

It is only by the grace of God that you are what you are and where you are (I Corinthians 15:10). You better tell somebody! I feel a shout coming on!

The grace that is upon you is from God the Father and Jesus Christ

I Corinthians 1:3

WARNING:
You can abuse grace and Christians can remove themselves from grace through disobedience and rebellion (I Timothy 4: 1-5; Hebrews 3:12).

Read Galatians 5:4 and write it in the space below:

_____

_____

_____

Who is the biblical example of someone falling from grace in Hebrews 12:16-17?

    a. Esau

    b. Paul

    c. Timothy

    d. John

As a person after God's own heart, running after Him daily, what are some things you can do through the grace that has been placed on you?

Use the following page to write out at least five things you can accomplish. Please provide scriptural support. For example, because God's grace is sufficient for me, I will lay hands on the sick and they shall recover (Mark 16:17).

Your turn:

_____

_____

_____

_____

It has been a week to treasure!

Week 5

GENERAL SESSION

Surrender

"Present your bodies a living sacrifice, holy, acceptable unto God, which is your reasonable service."
Romans 12:1

GENERAL SESSION
Surrender

SURRENDER! Just the sound of this word carries an element of stress for so many people. Yes, including believers. Sometimes we say we want God's will for our lives, but do we really mean that?

Okay, jog in place with me here. In your mind, think of me going into your house and labeling two of your rooms. Room #1 is labeled, The Will of God for Your Life, and Room #2 is labeled, Life Your Way. Upon completion of the labeling, I ask you to enter the room of your choice. What room do you think you would choose?

Complete the sentence: I would choose Room # _____.

If I did this at a number of believers' houses, what room do you think the majority of them would choose?

Complete the sentence: I think others would choose Room # _____.

I think most of us would like to think we would choose Room #1 but because of the fear of total surrender, many believers hold back. They are afraid if they surrender to God, He will ask them to do something with which they are not comfortable. I wish I could tell them that God would do no such thing, but I can't because that is exactly what He will ask them to do—something outside of their comfort zone. Why? Because it requires faith, and faith is what pleases Him.

Surrender is a trust issue. The room you choose is contingent upon who you trust the most with your life. Answering the following questions will help you make the quality choice to surrender to God. Who has my best interest at heart? Who will do what is best for me?

Surrendering to God means you will do what He says. It means to "let go" as well as to "let God." It means to obey God at all cost. Obedience is a major factor in this process. The Bible has many examples of people who obeyed God. Abraham is one such person.

Hebrews 11:8 says, **"By faith Abraham, when called to go to a place he would later receive as his inheritance, obeyed and went even though he did not know where he was going"** (NIV84).

Abraham lived in Ur of the Chaldeans, which was a very modern city during that time. Ur had a sophisticated culture. Abraham was not trying to leave Ur, especially to go to someplace unknown. I am sure Abraham was comfortable with his city and had planned a prosperous life for himself and his family. But God had other plans for Abraham. So what did Abraham do?

You are correct, he surrendered!

With your group, discuss and write at least three (3) things that God has revealed to you and you have totally obeyed. Write those three (3) things for each person in your group.

_____

_____

_____

_____

Now, discuss and write three (3) things that God has been dealing with you about but you have not obeyed…yet.

_____

_____

_____

_____

Revelations 4:11 says, **"You are worthy, our Lord and God, to receive glory and honor and power, for you created all things, and by your will they were created and have their being" (NIV84).**

It is very important to surrender to God's will for your life. This is what our week's study is all about. You will be enhanced as you capture the essence of surrender in these lessons. God is the ultimate source of all things. It is only befitting that you surrender to Him.

From the book *The Pursuit of God*, A.W. Tozer pens the following words:

"Every soul belongs to God and exists by His pleasure. God being Who and What He is, and we being who and what we are, the only thinkable relation between us is one of full Lordship on His part and complete submission on ours. We owe Him every honor that it is within our power to give Him. Our everlasting grief lies in giving Him anything less."

We are running a path charted for total surrender this week. I am excited about the journey. Thanks for joining me!

INDEPENDENT STUDY

Surrender

"Present your bodies a living sacrifice, holy, acceptable unto God, which is your reasonable service."
Romans 12:1

Week *Five*

Surrender

Day 1—"Thirst"

Talk about endurance! You have made it to week five and you are still running at a very good pace. Don't slow down just yet. Remember, proper breathing is the key. Use your abdominals! Abdominal breathing is the most efficient way to exchange oxygen and carbon dioxide. Let your stomach expand as you inhale and contract as you exhale. There you go! You are sure to make it to the finish line.

The focus of your path for this week is total surrender. Specifically for today, you will explore the concept of thirst and what it means to thirst after God and the things of God.

To jump start your run, let's define the word "thirst." According to *Webster's Dictionary*, thirst means having an eager desire; dry, parched, deficient in moisture. According to *Strong's Concordance*, thirst means to desire earnestly.

The word "thirst" is derived from the Greek word, *dipsao*. It is the same word that is used in the following scriptures: Psalm 42:1-2, 63:1; Matthew 5:6; John 19:28 and others.

The word "pants" (panteth in KJV) means to "long for."

Write Matthew 5:6 in the space provided below:

_____

_____

_____

Surrender

Read Psalm 42:1-2 and substitute the phrase "long for" wherever you see the word "pants" ("panteth" if you are reading the KJV). Then, substitute the phrase "desire earnestly" for the word "thirsts" ("thirsteth" if you are reading KJV). Then write the scripture below using the substitutions.

_____

_____

_____

_____

That makes it real, doesn't it? It paints a clearer picture of what the sons of Korah were feeling as they longed to worship God in the temples of Jerusalem.

Have you ever felt a longing (thirst) for the presence of God?

___ YES ___ NO

Describe what that felt like in the space provided.

_____

_____

_____

_____

At that time, were you in a dry place in your life? ___ YES ___ NO

What did you do to quench your thirst?

_____

_____

David found himself in a dry place in the wilderness of Judah as he was fleeing from people who sought to kill him. While in this place, he penned Psalm 63:1-2.

> *"O God, thou art my God; early will I seek thee: my soul thirsteth for thee, my flesh longeth for thee in a dry and thirsty land, where no water is; to see thy power and thy glory, so as I have seen thee in the sanctuary."*

One thing David did to quench his thirst for the presence of God was:

      a. He cried

      b. He sought God early

      c. He rested

      d. None of the above

The sons of Korah were thirsty for the presence of God. You get thirsty for the presence of God. David got thirsty for the presence of God.

Let's go deeper!

Read John 19:28 and tell who got thirsty for God's presence in this verse. _____

You are correct. Jesus got thirsty.

For years you may have read that scripture and pictured Jesus needing a gallon of water because He had been through so much. He had carried the cross through the streets and up Golgotha's Hill. He had been beaten, pierced in the side, had nails driven in his hands, and a crown of thorns pressed into His brow. He had been hanging on an old rugged cross in the heat for nine hours (Mark 15:33). Yes, Jesus needed and deserved water...to say the least. However, I also believe that Jesus was thirsty for His Father's presence. Before you stone me, listen. On the cross, Jesus became sin (2 Corinthians 5:21) for you and me, right? Well, at that particular time, God's presence was not with Jesus because God cannot look upon sin (Habakkuk 1:13). Jesus agonized because He had never been without the presence of God. Now for the first time, He was in a spiritual desert, a dry place.

Read and write Mark 15:34 in the space below.

_____

_____

_____

_____

The gospel of John picks up this scenario in chapter 19:28 by saying, **"After this, Jesus, knowing that all things were now accomplished...said, I thirst,"** I *dipsao!*

Shalom!

Week *Five*

Surrender

Day 2—"Thirst"

Psalm 143:6 says, **"I stretch forth my hands unto thee: my soul thirsteth after thee, as a thirsty land."**

Continuing where we left off yesterday, you acknowledged that in the quest after God, you can sometimes find yourself in a dry place—a place where it seems God's presence has left you and you become spiritually thirsty. You have this eager desire to touch Him, to get with Him, to feel the warmth of His love close up again. Well my friend, that could be a good place because one thing about being thirsty is that it is not something you can ignore. Thirst must be quenched or you can die of dehydration. A Biblical example of this is found in Genesis 21:14-19.

This scripture depicts the story of _____ in the wilderness with her son _____.

Hagar wept because Ishmael was _____.

Look at verse 19 and tell how God assisted Hagar in quenching the thirst of Ishmael.

_____

_____

_____

Some health experts say when you feel thirsty, you are already dehydrated. Additionally, they advise you drink water and not other things such as alcohol or caffeine, as these drinks do not help dehydration but instead add to it.

During the study today, you will learn or be reminded of what God says about those who thirst after Him. Thirsting for God is similar to thirsting in the natural. It is critical that you seek to quench this thirst.

Before you go any further, read John 4:13-14. Then read John 6:35. Does this present a contradiction in your mind regarding thirsting after God? If it didn't, you are a step ahead of where I was when I read it. But the Holy Spirit is always there to teach us. In this scripture, Jesus was speaking of unbelievers. For example, He told the woman at the well that she needed to drink from the fountain of living water. Jesus was saying He is the only permanent satisfaction for the human desire for life. He was speaking of Himself, because she was a Samaritan. Jews did not associate with Samaritans (John 4:9), because they were enemies. Samaritans did not worship the Living God. They were known for their blatant idolatry. One of the kings, who ruled in Samaria, was Ahab. Ahab was married to Jezebel, who worshipped Baal and killed the prophets of the Lord (I Kings, chapters 17 and 18).

In John 6:25-37, Jesus was talking to a group of people who did not believe in God at the time. As a matter of fact, in verse 28 they asked Jesus, "What shall we do, that we might work the works of God?" How did Jesus answer them in verse 29?

_____

_____

_____

In essence, after they had seen Jesus and the mighty works He was doing, they cultivated a thirst for God. He simply told them in verse

35 that if they would believe on Him, He would quench that thirst. In other words, He was the living water that quenched the thirst for knowing who God is.

Now, let's move on to see what happens when the believer thirsts for more of God, and see some things you can do to quench your thirst.

Look at Psalm 63:1-4. In this psalm, David said he was going to rise early and seek God so that he could see His power and glory in his present wilderness experience, just like he saw it in the sanctuary. He went on to say, **"Because your lovingkindness is better than life, my lips shall praise You. Thus will I bless you while I live" (NKJV).**

This paints a picture of what it looks like to surrender to God. David was demonstrating what to do when you, as a believer, get thirsty for more of God. Can't you just visualize him out there in the wilderness cuttin' a jig for Jesus? And check this out, David was running for his life. Yet he still praised God. He sought the Lord early.

Are you thirsty for more of God? _____ Yes _____ NO

Write Isaiah 44:3 in the space provided below.

_____

_____

_____

Jesus made this statement, "If anyone is thirsty, let him come to Me and drink." Where is this scripture found?

      a. John 7:36

      b. John 7:37

c. John 7:38

d. None of the above

We will end our run today with Matthew 5:6.

"Blessed are they which do hunger and _____ after righteous: for they shall be filled."

Week *Five*

Surrender

Day 3—"Hunger"

It's day three, yippie!! You are making wonderful progress on this track called "surrender." Hopefully you are well hydrated and warmed up for the run today. I am not anticipating steep hills, but there are a few curves up ahead. According to my running acumen, runners are challenged more when running curves because the inside leg does not get the ground reaction that is necessary to obtain maximum speed as compared to running on a straight path. Therefore, the maximum human running speed along a flat curved path is significantly slower relative to a straight path. I know you, my friend......you can handle both the straights and the curves.

Let's move into the lesson.

As you discuss the notion of spiritual hunger, it is quite possible to begin to sense divine hunger pangs. But that's okay. You are not the only one. You have a cadre of runners sharing your experience, me included. After you have built a reasonable foundation on Jesus Christ and the things of God, it is imperative that you continue to grow deeper in the things of God (Romans 1:17; 2 Corinthians 3:18). The need to grow in the things of God will keep you running after (seeking) Him, which in turn, will produce an insatiable hunger for more of Him.

Read Matthew 5:6 below. Underline the phrase that tells you what happens when you hunger after righteousness.

"Blessed are they which do hunger and thirst after righteousness: for they shall be filled."

Surrender

I love the way this scripture reads in The Message Bible and wanted to share it with you.

"You're blessed when you've worked up a good appetite for God. His food and drink is the best meal you will ever eat."

Hunger, like thirst, is not something that can be ignored for a long period of time. If you do not eat (physically or spiritually), guess what…you will die. Guaranteed!

Jesus expects you to hunger after the things of God. He also expects your appetite to increase from baby food to meat.

Read 1 Corinthians 3:1-3. Summarize the passage in the space provided.

_____

_____

_____

_____

Why is this scripture important in the study of hunger? When you don't hunger after the things of God, you become weak like a baby in Christ. Some things God can talk to you about and others He can't, because they may be too strong for you. That is not where He wants you to be.

Read Hebrews 5:12-14. What does this scripture say about those who have been walking with Jesus for a while and still want milk?

    a. They are unskillful in the word

    b. They are going to hell

c. They will be punished

d. None of the above

Did you get a sense that Jesus was pleased with this type of behavior?

_____ YES _____ NO

What does God do for His people who are experiencing hunger? See Psalm 107:9.

_____

_____

_____

God is no respecter of persons (Acts 10:34). If He satisfied the longing soul and filled them with goodness then, He will do the same for you today. Running after God is tantamount to an insatiable hunger for Him. In order to go deeper into the things of God for the purpose of being a better expression of Him and fulfilling the call of God on your life, it will require a sweet surrender to the hunger pangs. Not those that send you to Whataburger, but those that send you to the Word.

In John 4:34, what did Jesus say was His food? Write your answer below.

_____

_____

_____

The solution to spiritual hunger is spiritual:

a. appetite

b. food

c. water

d. friends

Write the words of Jesus found in John 6:41 in the space provided below.

_____

_____

_____

Read and write John 6:50.

_____

_____

_____

Jesus is the _____ of life (John 6:48).

You have done well. Divine Hunger + Divine Food = Divine Satisfaction, which will keep you running back for more of Him.

Bon Appetit!!

Week *Five*

Surrender

Day 4—"Spending Time with God"

Greetings to you on another beautiful day that the Lord has made! You have conquered the hills and the curves with a reasonable level of success. Look at you, progressing like a champion as you move forward in Him. He is pleased with you, my friend. He really is pleased with you!

Your run will continue today on the path of "surrender." You will explore the topic of "Spending Time with God." This is a familiar conversation to Christians all over the world. It is one that is taught in most of our churches. However, it is also one in which many believers struggle. I trust that our brief study regarding this topic will shed some light and help to dispel the religious bondage in which some have found themselves as it relates to spending time with God.

In actuality, God is omnipresent. He is everywhere. He is with you always (Matthew 28:20). Wherever you are and whatever you are doing right now, God is with you… but that does not mean you are with Him. Spending time with God involves you getting with Him and giving Him your undivided attention. To run this race successfully, you need more than "me time"— you need some "God time" as well. The purpose for this time is to help you build a personal relationship with Him. The key to building this relationship is communication and spending time together.

So, how do you do that? Good question! Ways to spend time with God include, but are not limited to: attending church, prayer, praise, worship, singing, reading the Bible, studying the Bible, helping others, encouraging others, giving, and taking the Lord's Supper.

For the duration of your run today, let's take a closer look at a few of these areas. Keep in mind that this lesson is not a condemnation session. No, the intent is to instruct in the ways of righteousness and keep us all focused on one message: RUNNING AFTER GOD!

Write Romans 8:1 in the space below.

_____

_____

_____

_____

Church – The church is basically a place where believers meet to hear the Word, encourage each other, pray, praise, worship, give, and partake of the Lord's Supper. It is very important for believers to gather together (Hebrews 10:24-25).

Note: According to scripture "the Church" that Jesus spoke about in Matthew 16:18 was not a building. It was and **is** a people. Read and write Matthew 16:18.

_____

_____

_____

_____

Read Ephesians 1:22-23. Fill in the blanks:

"And hath put all things under His feet, and gave him to be the head over all things to the _____, which is his _____, the _____ of him that filleth all in all."

The Church belongs to Jesus and is special to Him. It is likened to a bride of whom Jesus is the groom (Ephesians 5:25-27), and a branch with Jesus as the vine (John 15: 1). It is also pictured as a flock of sheep with Jesus as the shepherd (John 10:7-27). It is seen as a temple with Jesus as the cornerstone (1 Peter 2:5). It is described as ministering priests with Jesus as the High Priest (1 Peter 2:5-9) and it is explained as a new creation with Jesus as the head and first fruits (1 Corinthians 15:45).

How did Jesus come into ownership of the Church? See Acts 20:28.

_____

_____

_____

_____

To reiterate, the church building is where the local church gathers (Hebrews 10:24-25) to edify one another, study the Bible, pray, praise, worship, give, administer the ordinances of the Lord, baptism and the Lord's Supper. Additionally, through this local assembly, the Church is responsible for evangelizing the world (Mark 16:15).

Studying the Word – In spending time with God, this is major. Most of what we know about God comes from the Word of God. You cannot know God apart from His Word. He and the Word are one (John 1:1). It is imperative that you take time to get into the Word on a regular basis. You can do that by listening to CDs and studying along. You can do exactly what you are doing right now—participating in a home Bible study course. You can subscribe to a Bible Reading Plan. You can purchase a One-Year Bible that takes you through the Bible in one year. You can study by topics such as faith, healing, love, etc. You can do a character study and more. The key is you must do it. You have time!

You know the scripture. Write II Timothy 2:15:

_____

_____

_____

_____

Giving – I was almost intimidated to talk about this topic. The scriptures have much to say regarding giving, even though many people have been misled and confused regarding it. The Bible is very clear on this subject. Luke 6:38 tells us to **"Give and it shall be given unto you, good measure, pressed down, shaken together and running over."** Mark 10:29-30 says whatever we give for the gospel's sake, we will receive a hundred-fold return now and in this time. However, I believe the ground rule for giving is that all giving must be done from the heart. Look at II Corinthians 9:7 and fill in the blanks:

"Every man according as he purposeth _____ _____ _____, **so let him** _____; **not** _____, **or of** _____: **for** _____ **loveth a** _____ **giver."**

Giving is the plan that God instituted to bless our lives. This plan includes, but is not limited to:

- ❖ seedtime and harvest – Genesis 8:22
- ❖ sowing and reaping – Galatians 6:7; II Corinthians 9:6-8
- ❖ giving and receiving – Philippians 4:10-19
- ❖ tithes and offering – Malachi 3:8-12

Prayer, Praise, and Worship – Spend time in prayer, praise and worship every day. God loves to hear our praises. We discussed this at length in week two. Refer back to week Two – Day 3 and answer the following:

There are many types of prayer. Name three of them and give their meaning. For example: Thanksgiving – gratitude.

Your turn:

_____

_____

_____

_____

Never get in bondage regarding the time of day or length of time you pray. Ask the Holy Spirit to help you develop endurance and stamina in prayer. Talk to your heavenly Father from your heart everyday and listen as He talks back. On some days, you may have more time than others, and that's okay.

Let me caution you. Stay clear of the idea that you don't have time to spend with God. You have time to spend with Him. Just think, He gives you 24 hours every day. He never gives anyone else more time than He gives you. He made time for just for you, so include Him in on some of it.

Be creative!

- ❖ Get up a few minutes earlier.
- ❖ When you are using the restroom, pray in the spirit or sing to Him.
- ❖ While driving to and from work, listen to the Word, pray, and praise.
- ❖ Take three minute "Praise Breaks" during the day.
- ❖ While cooking, you can pray and praise or listen to the Word.
- ❖ Acknowledge Him in the middle of what you are doing. Talk to Him.
- ❖ Mowing the yard is a perfect time to talk to Him.

See you tomorrow!

Week *Five*

Surrender

Day 5—"Hearing His Voice"

You have made it to the end of another week. Five weeks have flown by already! Endurance is surely your strong suit! Today, you will wrap up a week of surrender. You have thirst, hungered, spent time with Him and now you will hear His voice.

Before moving on into the study, stop and pray. Ask God to help you hear from Him today. Cover yourself with the blood of Jesus and surrender to the guidance of the Holy Spirit. Praise the Lord!

Hearing the voice of God has always been a carefully taught subject. It's the type of conversation that more often than not, has hanging over it the fear of making a mistake and getting the voice of the devil confused with the voice of God.

Read II Timothy 1:7. Fill in the blanks.

"For God hath not given us the spirit of _____; but of _____, and of _____, and of a sound mind."

Let's just put this out on the table. God is not spooky. He does not sound like the Wizard of Oz when He speaks to you. God is not mean and hateful, nor is He waiting for you to make a mistake so He can kill you. God loves you. He only wants the best for you. He is not counting up all of your mistakes and shortcomings to use them against you. He desires to fellowship with you. He wants some quiet time with you so that in the stillness of your soul, you can hear His voice.

Write Job 33:14 below:

_____

_____

_____

_____

There are many voices that want your attention: the voice of others, the voice of your flesh, the voice of the devil, the voice of reasoning, and others. These voices compete with the voice of God, which in some instances, causes confusion for the believer. Read John 10:27. What did Jesus say about His sheep?

_____

_____

_____

_____

Don't try to misunderstand that. It is exactly as He said. You know His voice. You have heard it and many times obeyed it. God's voice does not thunder through the sky or speak like Alfred Hitchcock when you are in your bed at night. Many times, His voice comes as spontaneous thoughts, ideas, impressions and on occasion, He might speak audibly in your spirit.

How did Elijah describe God's voice in I Kings 19:12?

_____

_____

Read and explain John 8:47.

_____
_____
_____
_____

Let's go deeper!

Habakkuk 2:1 says, **"I will stand upon my watch, and set me upon the tower, and will watch to see what he will say unto me, and what I shall answer when I am reproved."**

This is a clear picture of someone listening for the voice of God. There are secrets to hearing the voice of God embedded in this scripture. Let's look closely.

- ❖ He kept his time with God.
- ❖ He was in a quiet place, away from distractions.
- ❖ He waited to hear from God.
- ❖ He anticipated a conversation and what his response would be.

What did God say to Habakkuk?

_____
_____
_____
_____

Surrender

In order for Habakkuk to hear God, he had to get quiet. He had to go to a place and allow his own thoughts and emotions to subside. This is almost a curse word to some people. But yes, you must tune out the noise of life to tune into what God is saying.

What does Psalm 46:10 instruct you to do?

_____

_____

_____

_____

When you get your flesh and mind quiet, you will begin to experience an inner knowing, or spontaneous flow, of thoughts in your spirit that come up through your mind. An excellent way to get into this place is to listen to worship music or sing to the Lord.

Here are a few helpful hints:

- ❖ If your mind begins to wander off on things you need to do, take a moment and write those things down. This will dismiss them from your thoughts.
- ❖ If you sense you need to repent about something, stop and do so.
- ❖ Once you have taken care of the issues, begin to focus on Jesus (Hebrews 12:2).
- ❖ Share your heart with Him.
- ❖ As you share your heart with Him, He will begin to share with you.
- ❖ Journal what you hear.

- ❖ If you feel that God is speaking a message to you but you are not really sure if it is from God, here are some good questions to ask yourself:
- ❖ Does it line up with the written Scriptures?
- ❖ Does it lead you into a closer relationship with God, a greater unity with Him?
- ❖ Does it cause greater humility in you, and a greater dependence upon God?
- ❖ Does it cause greater love, joy, and peace from God in you?

I want you to end the run for this week with this thought from I Corinthians 14:33: **"For God is not the author of confusion, but of peace."**

Let peace be your guide as you listen for the voice of God. If you feel peace, continue. If you feel confused, stop.

Thanks for running with me this week!

Week 6

GENERAL SESSION

Reflections

"Then shall the righteous shine forth as the sun."
Matthew 13:43

GENERAL SESSION
Reflections

This week, we will explore what it means to be reflections of the Most High God. The foundational scripture is Matthew 13:43, **"Then shall the righteous shine forth as the sun in the kingdom of their Father. Who hath ears to hear, let him hear."**

The topics will include:

- ❖ Arise and Shine
- ❖ Light
- ❖ Love
- ❖ Love – Your Neighbor
- ❖ Love – Yourself

The word "reflect" means to show forth, to demonstrate, and to express the image of a person or object so that it can be seen by all. Matthew 15:31 says, **"Insomuch that the multitude wondered, when they saw the dumb to speak, the maimed to be whole, the lame to walk, and the blind to see: and they glorified the God of Israel."**

This is a vivid picture of what we mean by reflections. Being a reflection of something or someone usually takes on an external manifestation. The Bible tells us that our purpose as believers in Christ is to be conformed into His image so that we can reflect His character and attributes in all we do. **"For whom He did foreknow, He also did predestinate to be conformed to the image of His Son"** (Romans 8:29).

A genuine external reflection of our God and His love for mankind is what is needed to turn the hearts of the world towards Him. Nancy

Missler, a Bible scholar, penned these words, "Seeing living examples of Jesus is what will bring our sons and daughters, our friends and acquaintances to the Lord. When they see real love, hear His supernatural wisdom and experience His power through us, they'll know that *yes, Jesus is real. He is alive. And He cares*! Nothing will bring others to the saving knowledge of Christ faster than seeing genuine living examples. And nothing will turn them away quicker than phoniness and hypocrisy. Therefore, glorifying, manifesting and reflecting Christ in everything is our highest attainment in this life."

God is vitally concerned with the witness our life leaves with the world around us! Our life is constantly sending a message to those around us and it isn't what we *say* with our mouth that is our witness, but it is more a combination of what we say, how we say it, and what we do.

The Biblical word "witness" does not necessarily mean to speak, but rather, it has the meaning of our life being a reflection of God's glory to the world around us. This word "witness" means to display, such as a famous basketball player displaying his trophies. "Exhibit" is another word that further expresses the word "witness."

Reflecting God's glory will involve people. Treating God's people right is paramount to reflecting His glory. John 3:16 says **"For God so loved the world...."** He was not talking about the geographical landscape of planet earth. No, He was referring to people. God loves people and if you are going to be a reflection of Him, guess what? You will have to love people as well. There is no getting around that. Even those who are hard to love—love them anyway!

I believe God wants us to stop talking the Word so much and start living it. Write Galatians 6:10 in the space provided:

_____

_____

_____

_____

Isaiah 60:1-2 is one of my most favorite passages in the Bible and probably the reason why we have the chapter of "Reflections" in this study.

> *"Arise, shine; for thy light is come, and the glory of the LORD is risen upon thee. For, behold, the darkness shall cover the earth, and gross darkness the people: but the LORD shall arise upon thee, and his glory shall be seen upon thee."*

Does this scripture foster the notion that it is imperative for believers in Christ to reflect Him? _____ YES _____ NO

Before we conclude our General Session, read Isaiah 60:1-2 again and summarize the passage in your own words in the space provided.

_____

_____

_____

_____

I am looking forward to another awesome week of running after God. Thanks for being my partner.

Shalom!

Week *Six*

Reflections

Day 1—"Arise and Shine"

You have made it to week six, which is the final week of this study. That is terrific! The run this week will be done in five-day sprints. Sprinting improves speed, strength, and agility. It is all about power and efficiency. Your power output is critical to success on the track this week. Get ready, set, go!

Let's review the foundational scripture of Matthew 13:43: **"Then shall the righteous shine forth as the sun in the kingdom of their Father. Who hath ears to hear, let him hear."**

The righteous are those who are in right standing with God through Jesus Christ. That's you and me. Second Corinthians 5:21 says, **"For He hath made him to be sin for us, who knew no sin; that we might be made the righteousness of God in him."**

This scripture is talking about the righteous. These are people who will:

    a. shine forth as the sun

    b. pant like a deer

    c. preach like Paul

    d. none of the above

Write a definition for the word "shine" in the space provided.

_____

_____

_____

_____

Great! Did your definition include such phrases as: to reflect light, to be conspicuous or distinguished? _____ YES _____ NO

Read Isaiah 60:1-2 below.

"Arise and shine; for thy light is come, the glory of the LORD is risen upon thee. For behold, the darkness shall cover the earth, and gross darkness the people: but the LORD shall arise upon thee, and His glory shall be seen upon thee."

Isaiah, affectionately known as the "evangelical prophet," is speaking specifically about the nation of Israel and prophetically about the Church. To Israel, he is saying your Redeemer is coming, arise. To the modern Church, he is saying your Redeemer has come, so arise.

The word "arise" comes from the Greek word *quwm*, (pronounced koom), which means to rise and is used in context of lifting a suffering woman (Israel—see Isaiah 3:26) from the ashes of mourning. Quwm has also been translated in the King James Version as one who is given clarity, been roused to activity, ordained or strengthened. Dr. Creflo Dollar defines the word "arise" as to get up, change your posture and your position.

You can see another example of this word being used in Isaiah 52:1-2. Read these scriptures and tell what stands out in your mind.

_____

_____

_____

While perusing these scriptures some years ago, I was totally flabbergasted by the urgent request to the church: "Wake up, wake up!" These scriptures are specifically speaking to the people of God. In my "holier-than-thou" mind, I thought certainly the church is not asleep. If anybody is asleep, it must be the world. Well to be truthful, I was perusing these scriptures because I had a strong impression to get my Bible and read. I knew God wanted to say something to me specifically. I felt led to turn to this scripture, not knowing what it said. As I began to read, I heard the words "Wake up," like someone with authority was telling *me* to wake up. So again, "holier-than-thou" me asked, "God, are You telling me to wake up?" Of course, you know the answer.

Did you know that you could be in bondage and not be aware of it?
_____ YES _____ NO

No matter how much you currently know, you still have a lot to learn.

Continue reading Isaiah 52:1-6. Concentrate on verse 4. What do you think the word "Egypt" symbolizes? Circle your answer.

    a. A far away land

    b. Bondage

    c. Freedom

    d. None of the above

You are a deep thinker! I agree with you. Egypt symbolizes bondage, slavery, and captivity. Read Exodus 13:14 to validate your response.

When God's people, Israel, were in bondage, He told Moses to go down to Egypt and tell Pharaoh to let His people go. After God's people were free, they forgot who they were and what God had done for them. Eventually, they ended up in captivity again.

The scripture in Isaiah points to the coming of Jesus. This is good news for Israel as well as the Church. Read Isaiah 60:1. Re-write this verse using Dr. Creflo Dollar's definition for arise.

_____

_____

_____

_____

Could this scripture be saying there is a better posture and higher position for you than you are currently experiencing? ___ YES ___ NO

My friend, assume your position!

Week *Six*

Reflections

Day 2—"Light"

It's a new day and I am excited about running with you. Remember, this is a week of power sprints. You will continue your study on Reflections and its different aspects and analogies. Today you will delve into the phenomenon of light. Get ready to shine!

Your foundational scriptures are Matthew 13:43 and Isaiah 60:1-2. Please read them below.

Matthew 13:43: **"Then shall the righteous shine forth as the sun in the kingdom of their Father."**

Isaiah 60:1-2: **"Arise and shine; for thy light is come, and the glory of the LORD is risen upon thee. For, behold, the darkness shall cover the earth, and gross darkness the people: but the LORD shall arise upon thee, and His glory shall be seen upon thee."**

Yesterday's lesson encompassed a lengthy discussion of the word "arise." One meaning of this word was to "get up, change your posture and your position." When you see the word "arise" in Scripture, many times there is a conjunction connecting it to another action. More often than not, the action is something you were not previously doing. It is unusual to hear the command to arise without a connected action. Let's take a look at a few examples before you move on.

Genesis 13:17: **"Arise, walk through the land in the length of it and in the breadth of it; for I will give it unto thee."**

I Samuel 16:12: **"And the LORD said, Arise, anoint him: for this is he."**

Mark 2:11: **"I say unto thee, Arise, and take up thy bed, and go thy way into thine house."**

Look at Isaiah 60:1 and tell what action you are expected to take after you arise? Complete the sentence in first person.

I am expected to _____.

Why do you think you are expected to shine? (See Matthew 5:14.)

_____

_____

_____

_____

According to Isaiah 60:1, what causes you to reflect light? Explain.

_____

_____

_____

What do Matthew 5:15 and Isaiah 60:2 have as a common thread?

    a. You are a shining star

    b. Your light gives light to others

    c. You are to be praised

    d. None of the above

Reflections

Light has always been important to God. One of His first creations was light (Genesis 1:3). First John 1:5 tells us that God is light. James 1:17 describes God as the Father of Lights. Matthew 4:12-16 refers to Jesus as the Great Light. Psalm 119:105 reveals God's Word is light and Matthew 5:14 says you are light.

Write Philippians 2:15 in the space provided below.

_____

_____

_____

_____

When God created light in Genesis chapter one, what was its purpose?

      a. To eradicate the natural darkness that was on the earth

      b. So He could see Himself

      c. To see the dinosaurs

      d. All of the above

When God sent Jesus (the Great Light) to the earth, what was His purpose?

      a. To eradicate the spiritual darkness (sin) of the world

      b. To test Joseph's heart

      c. To perform the Last Supper

      d. None of the above

Let's end our sprint today with this confession:

I arise and shine because my light has come and the glory of the Lord has risen upon me. Though darkness covers the earth and gross darkness the people, the glory of the Lord shall be seen upon me. Sinners will come to Jesus because of the light of His glory that radiates from me.

Shalom, Shalom!!

Week *Six*

Reflections

Day 3—"Love"

It's a marvelous day to continue our run together. You have done a knock out job with keeping the pace. The big idea for today will center on the subject of love. Yes, love! It is the greatest attribute of the Father that you have been commanded to reflect. So lace up your shoes and let's get started.

The backdrop for today's power sprint will hover around Matthew 22: 34-40.

> *"But when the Pharisees had heard that he had put the Sadducees to silence, they were gathered together. Then one of them, which was a lawyer, asked him a question, tempting him, and saying, Master, which is the great commandment in the law? Jesus said unto him, Thou shalt love the Lord thy God with all thy heart, and with all thy soul, and with all thy mind. This is the first and great commandment. And the second is like unto it, Thou shalt love thy neighbour as thyself. On these two commandments hang all the law and the prophets."*

Write the greatest commandment in the space below:

_____

_____

_____

_____

What snatches your attention the most about this commandment?

_____

_____

_____

_____

The Hebrew word for "heart" is *lebab*, which means to be enclosed—as the interior or center, hence, the heart. In the Greek, the word is *kardia*. It means the seat in the center of man's inward life—the place of human depravity or the sphere of divine influence. Both meanings point to that which gives man "life."

"Heart" also means the real you that will live on through eternity. It's the "you" that lives inside of your body. According to 1 Thessalonians 5:23, you are three parts: You are a **spirit** that lives inside of a **body** and you possess a **soul**.

I am curious. How do you love God with all of your heart? Explain.

_____

_____

_____

_____

Wow! That's an awesome response!

In light of the scripture and the literal definitions of the word "heart," I agree with you. To love God with all your heart simply means to love Him with your whole being, with your life. Your highest objective in life is to love Him with all that you are and all that you have.

Everything you do should be congruent with His will and way, as He is the object of your affection.

I want you to see another part of Matthew 22:37 that says we are to love God with all our mind. The mind really is a terrible thing to waste! God gave you a mind so you can think, imagine, and be creative just like Him. As a believer, you are told in Romans 12:2 to renew your mind. The mind is important and as you use your renewed mind, you reflect His glory. Read and write I Corinthians 2:16 in the space below:

_____

_____

_____

_____

You have the mind of Christ. That means whatever is needed in your sphere of influence, you have the potential of coming up with the solutions. If books, inventions, or discoveries are needed, they are in you. That's why God has you there. When you allow yourself to imagine and be creative in your assigned place, you reflect His glory. You are loving Him with your mind.

What problem in your workplace or area of influence stands out in your mind?

_____

_____

_____

_____

What can you do so that the glory of God could be seen there?

_____

_____

_____

_____

When will you begin?

_____

_____

Refer back to Matthew 22:34-40 found at the beginning of this chapter.

Jesus told the religious people that the greatest commandment was to love God with all your heart, soul, and mind. He added that there was another commandment equal to that one. Write that commandment in the space below.

_____

_____

_____

_____

In your biblically educated opinion, is loving your neighbor equal to loving God? _____ YES _____ NO

Explain.

_____

_____

_____

_____

We will continue tomorrow.

Love!

Week *Six*

Reflections

Day 4—"Love – Your Neighbor"

You will continue your run by picking up where you left off on Day Three. For real this time, it's going to be a power sprint! Ready, Go!

Matthew 22:39 says, **"And the second is like unto it, thou shalt love thy neighbor as thyself."**

We are still discussing being a reflection of God in the earth arena. You have covered information regarding the following: Arise and Shine, Light, and The Greatest Commandment (Love – God). Today, you will make a deeper incision into the greatest commandment, which we learned is two-fold: Love the Lord with all your heart, soul, and mind and love your neighbor as yourself.

Is Jesus serious? Does He really expect for you to love your neighbor as yourself? YES! It is not a suggestion, He made it a commandment! Not only that, but it is the centerpiece of the commandments. It is a requirement for all Christians. The question arises, "Who is your neighbor?" Read Luke 10:25-37. Write your definition for "neighbor" in the space below.

_____

_____

_____

_____

Good answer!

In looking at this parable, you understand that three people saw the man in the ditch: the preacher, the Levite, and the Samaritan. All three of these people knew this man needed help.

Did the priest help the man? _____ YES _____ NO

Explain.

_____

_____

_____

_____

Did the Levite help him? _____ YES _____ NO

Explain.

_____

_____

_____

_____

The third person to pass by was a Samaritan. Samaritans in those days were foreigners scorned by the Jews for unorthodox customs. What did the Samaritan do differently from the other two travelers?

a. He checked to see if he knew the man

b. He looked beyond customs, rituals, and rules to help someone in need

c. He checked to see if he could get any media attention for doing a good deed

d. None of the above

Have you ever missed an opportunity to help someone?

___ YES ___ NO

What was the reason?

a. Too busy

b. Suspicious

c. They weren't a member of your church

d. Other _____

You are not alone; I have missed many opportunities as well.

Let's pray.

Father, in the name of Jesus, I confess that I have not loved my neighbor as myself on occasions. I ask You to forgive me and to help me to be more of a reflection of You in this area, in Jesus' name, Amen.

You don't have to like your neighbor, but Jesus has commanded you to love him. Loving your neighbor as yourself may require you to ask two questions:

1. What would Jesus do in this situation?
2. What if I were the man lying in the ditch, how would I want to be treated?

Your neighbor is not only the person who lives next door but also:

    a. the hurting

    b. the lost

    c. the poor

    d. all of the above

Shalom!

Week *Six*

Reflections

Day 5—"Love – Yourself"

Let's continue from yesterday. One of the problems with loving our neighbors as ourselves is the fact that some of us don't love ourselves. We don't like the way we look. We don't like our skin color. We don't like our size…and so on.

Today, you will take a powerful sprint down the track of "Loving Yourself Avenue." I know this is not a popular subject, but definitely one that must be addressed.

Read Matthew 22:34-40 again.

"But when the Pharisees had heard that he had put the Sadducees to silence, they were gathered together. Then one of them, which was a lawyer, asked him a question, tempting him, and saying, Master, which is the great commandment in the law? Jesus said unto him, Thou shalt love the Lord thy God with all thy heart, and with all thy soul, and with all thy mind. This is the first and great commandment. And the second is like unto it, Thou shalt love thy neighbour as thyself. On these two commandments hang all the law and the prophets."

Write Matthew 22:39 in the space below.

_____

_____

_____

Reflections

In your opinion, is this verse saying you have to love yourself first in order to know how to love your neighbor? _____ YES _____ NO

Who is speaking in this verse? _____

When Jesus tells you to do something, that means it is important and will benefit the kingdom (others as well as yourself). _____True_____False

Would you agree there are many reasons why people don't love themselves? ___ Yes ____ NO

Cite some of those reasons:

_____

_____

_____

_____

Did your list include things like traumatic childhood, victimization (rape, abuse, domestic violence), poor parenting, unhealthy role models, negative self-thoughts and self-talk, to name a few?

If this is you or someone you know, let's put an end to this awful nightmare. You are to love yourself, not in a prideful or arrogant kind of way, but in accordance to what God says about you. You cannot expect others to love you if you don't love yourself. Often, people who feel rejected by others are the ones who brought the spirit of rejection to the relationship in the first place. Rejection is circular.

You reject you ➡ You send that message out to your world through words and actions ➡ Those words and actions produce the negative energy of rejection around you ➡ Which returns multiplied to you through the principle of seedtime and harvest, and the law of natural attraction.

I have several questions for you:

- ❖ Do you think you are unworthy?
- ❖ Do you see all your mistakes and sins?
- ❖ Do you express what is bad about you before others get a chance to do so?
- ❖ Do you call yourself names?
- ❖ Do you compare yourself to others and feel you come up short?
- ❖ Do you struggle to see the good in you?
- ❖ Do you feel rejected by others on a regular basis?
- ❖ Do you look for love in all the wrong places?

Did you answer "yes" to any of these questions? Don't worry, my friend, you will get victory in this area, beginning now. Let's look into the Word of God to prove that you are accepted, secure, and significant in Jesus Christ. It does not matter what anyone else says or does. Allow the Word of God to be final authority in your life.

- ❖ You are God's child – John 1:12
- ❖ You are a friend of Jesus – John 15:15
- ❖ You have been bought with a price – I Corinthians 6:19
- ❖ You are chosen by God – I Peter 5:9
- ❖ You are complete in Christ – Colossians 2:9-10
- ❖ You are free from condemnation – Romans 8:1

- ❖ You cannot be separated from the love of God – Romans 8:31-39
- ❖ You have a spirit of power, love and a sound mind – 2 Timothy 1:7
- ❖ You are born of God and the evil one cannot touch you – I John 5:18
- ❖ You are God's workmanship – Ephesians 2:10
- ❖ You can do ALL things through Christ, Who strengthens you – Philippians 4:19

So, how do you begin to love yourself again?

- ❖ Find out what God's Word says about you.
- ❖ Begin to speak the Word over yourself.
- ❖ Begin to act like the words you speak are true.
- ❖ Forgive others.
- ❖ Forgive yourself.
- ❖ Appreciate who you are.
- ❖ Move forward. Do not live in the past.
- ❖ Take control of your thought life. Replace self-defeating thoughts with the truth about you.
- ❖ Be thankful and appreciate the people and other blessings in your life.
- ❖ Begin to affirm others.
- ❖ Believe that you are wonderful and unique.

Write Psalm 139:14 in the space below:

_____

_____

_____

_____

Read Psalm 139:1-18. Develop a personal confession from this Psalm and write it in the space provided.

O lord, thou hast searched me, and known me.

Thou knowest my downsitting and mine uprising, thou understandest my thought afar off.

Thou compassest my path and my lying down, and art acquainted with all my ways.

For there is not a word in my tongue, but, lo, O LORD, thou knowest it altogether.

Thou hast beset me behind and before, and laid thine hand upon me.

Such knowledge is too wonderful for me; it is high, I cannot attain unto it.

Whither shall I go from thy spirit? or whither shall I flee from thy presence?

If I ascend up into heaven, thou art there: if I make my bed in hell, behold, thou art there.

If I take the wings of the morning, and dwell in the uttermost parts of the sea;

Even there shall thy hand lead me, and thy right hand shall hold me.

If I say, Surely the darkness shall cover me; even the night shall be light about me.

Yea, the darkness hideth not from thee; but the night shineth as the day: the darkness and the light are both alike to thee.

For thou hast possessed my reins: thou hast covered me in my mother's womb.

I will praise thee; for I am fearfully and wonderfully made: marvelous are thy works; and that my soul knoweth right well.

My substance was not hid from thee, when I was made in secret, and curiously wrought in the lowest parts of the earth.

Thine eyes did see my substance, yet being unperfect; and in thy book all my members were written, which in continuance were fashioned, when as yet there was none of them.

How precious also are thy thoughts unto me, O God! how great is the sum of them!

If I should count them, they are more in number than the sand: when I awake, I am still with thee.

My Personal Confession about "Me"

_____

_____

_____

_____

_____

_____

_____

I have thoroughly enjoyed running with you. My life has been enriched by your presence and participation. Continue to love God and run after Him with all your heart.

Shalom!

ABOUT THE AUTHOR

Dr. Josie Washington Carr is an author, educator, entrepreneur, and inspirational speaker. She is the CEO of DESTINY Educational Consulting Group and the President and Founder of Success You-niversity, 7M Stilettos Foundation, Believers United for Successful Schools, The Prayer Connection, and Jostan Community, Incorporated.

She has authored several books: The Impact of Inclusion on Academic Achievement, Inspire for Teachers, iGod, The Believers Passport to a Fulfilled Life, Rise to Your Destiny: A Divine Mandate, and The Healing Chronicle.

Dr. Carr was formally educated at University of Houston and Texas Southern University in Houston, Texas, where she received a B. S. in Physical Education, M. Ed. in Special Education, M. Ed. in Mid-Management and a Doctorate of Education in Educational Administration. She has served as a teacher, counselor, principal, Executive Director of Education and educational consultant. Additionally she is a graduate of Light Christian College of Ministry and Ministry Development Institute in Houston, Texas.

Dr. Carr is a committed member of El Shaddai International Christian Centre, pastored by Dr. Ramson and Pastor Estrella Mumba.

She is the wife of Dr. Stanley B. Carr and the proud mother of Jarvis and Jakia Carr.

PRAYER OF SALVATION

God loves you—no matter who you are, no matter what your past. God loves you so much that He gave His one and only begotten Son for you. The Bible tells us that "...whoever believes in Him shall not perish but have eternal life" (John 3:16 NIV). Jesus laid down His life and rose again so that we could spend eternity with Him in heaven and experience His absolute best on earth. If you would like to receive Jesus into your life, say the following prayer out loud and mean it from your heart.

Heavenly Father, I come to You admitting that I am a sinner. Right now, I choose to turn away from sin, and I ask You to cleanse me of all unrighteousness. I believe that Your Son, Jesus, died on the cross to take away my sins. I also believe that He rose again from the dead so that I might be forgiven of my sins and made righteous through faith in Him. I call upon the name of Jesus Christ to be the Savior and Lord of my life. Jesus, I choose to follow You and ask that You fill me with the power of the Holy Spirit. I declare that right now I am a child of God. I am free from sin and full of the righteousness of God. I am saved in Jesus' name. Amen.

If you prayed this prayer to receive Jesus Christ as your Savior for the first time, please contact us on the Web at **www.harrisonhouse.com** to receive a free book.

Or you may write to us at
Harrison House • P.O. Box 35035 • Tulsa, Oklahoma 74153

The Harrison House Vision

Proclaiming the truth and the power

Of the Gospel of Jesus Christ

With excellence;

Challenging Christians to

Live victoriously,

Grow spiritually,

Know God intimately.

www.ingramcontent.com/pod-product-compliance
Lightning Source LLC
LaVergne TN
LVHW051056080426
835508LV00019B/1908